MIND GAMES
Mental Fitness for Tennis

To Greg

Good luck with your game
— and mind games too!

[signature]

Jason Whitmore won the Kent County Short Tennis Doubles Championship in the UK when he was eight and the Kent County Tennis Singles Championship for boys under twelve. He has attended several tennis camps in the United States, including spending three months at Nick Bollettieri's Tennis Academy. He is also an excellent skier and table tennis player and he won a sports scholarship to his present school. He will be fifteen at the time of publication. His many interests include snow boarding, roller blading, basketball, acting, films, Newcastle United, and just hanging out with friends.

John Whitmore was a professional racing driver in the 1960s during which he won both the British and European Saloon Car Championships. He studied the new psychologies in the United States, trained with Tim Gallwey, author of *The Inner Game of Tennis*, and returned to England in 1980 to found tennis and ski schools based on *inner game* principles. He is now a business management consultant, specialising in performance coaching and culture change. He has written several books on personal, social and skill development, including the 100,000 copy bestseller *Coaching for Performance*, and more recently, *Need, Greed or Freedom* (Element Books).

MIND GAMES
Mental Fitness for Tennis

Jason and John Whitmore

ELEMENT
CHILDREN'S BOOKS

SHAFTESBURY, DORSET · BOSTON, MASSACHUSETTS · MELBOURNE, VICTORIA

First published in Great Britain 1998
by Element Children's Books
The Old School House
The Courtyard, Bell Street
Shaftesbury, Dorset SP7 8BP

Published in the USA in 1998 by Element Books, Inc.
160 North Washington Street, Boston, MA 02114.

Published in Australia in 1998 by Element Books Ltd and
distributed by Penguin Books Australia Ltd, 487
Maroondah Highway, Ringwood, Victoria 3134.

British Library Cataloging in Publication data available.
Library of Congress Cataloguing in Publication data
available.

ISBN 1-901881-709
10 9 8 7 6 5 4 3 2 1

Printed and bound in Great Britain
by Creative Print and Design Wales, Ebbw Vale

CONTENTS

FOREWORD

Many adult tennis players who played tournament tennis as juniors will wish that this book had been read by their parents at the time. Sean Brawley, who was ranked in the top ten in US junior tennis, played number one for the University of Southern California, and ranked in the top 150 on the Association of Tennis Professionals (ATP) Tour, said he didn't find joy in playing the game until his thirties when he read *The Inner Game of Tennis* which enabled him to let go of the external pressures that burden most competitive players. 'If I had been told it was OK to play for myself and follow my own aspirations instead of those of my father, my experience of the game and even my results would have been much better,' Brawley said after reading *Mind Games*.

Clearly, something is amiss with the way adults teach and manage junior sports of all kinds. When parents attempt to live out their own ambitions through their children, it creates one of the most detrimental pressures in junior tennis. Such pressures not only can take the fun out of the game, but tragically interfere with the many beneficial learning processes otherwise available to the junior player.

Ever since working with John Whitmore in the 1970s, I have been impressed by his grasp of the inner game principles as demonstrated in tennis and skiing clinics as well as in his management training programmes. Both Sean and I spent some court time with Jason in California last summer and I saw his promise then. Now, the Whitmores' *Mind Games* shows that together father and son have attained a rare collaborative understanding of the critical aspect of the game that takes place in the head of the player.

If read thoughtfully and applied, this book can help other families to bring some sanity to competitive tennis. Perhaps most importantly, it poses the rarely asked question, 'Why do you play the game?' Bringing this question into the open gives both player and parent a conscious choice in the matter and, thus, the chance to avoid the prevailing confusion surrounding the meaning of winning and achievement in modern sports.

Ultimately, any junior player struggles to gain control – not just of the ball and racket but of his or her own mind and emotions. Parents who over-control make this job harder and invite the junior into over-controlling mental habits in their performance. The alternative is learning how to think for oneself, make one's own mistakes and find the fun that can only come when one is truly playing for oneself. Then players can find a natural way to gain access to and develop inherent capabilities that they can take with them through life. No matter how many trophies line the mantle, the gold to be mined by all players is the focus, confidence, and determination that will serve them well in all future endeavours.

Sean Brawley who is now the leading inner game professional in the US knows that the methods and perspective represented in this book work. 'I can only hope,' he says, 'that the reader will attempt to apply these fundamental natural laws of learning on the tennis court as well as off. Experience, not words will be your greatest teacher.'

Tim Gallwey

PART I

JASON'S STORY

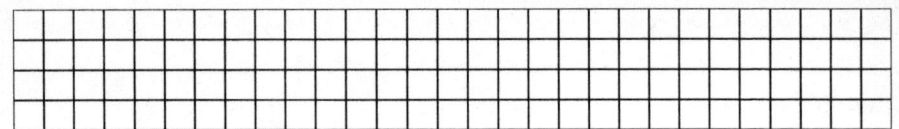

Introduction

The mind is key, but where is the key to the mind?

This book is for aspiring young tennis players from eight to eighteen and beyond, and for their parents and coaches. It is not about technique, tactics or physical fitness, although it touches on each of them; it is about developing the mental skills which bind all three. It is about coping with the pressures and obstacles, and avoiding the pitfalls a young player is likely to meet as he or she progresses.

If you play tennis or intend to, and since you have continued to read beyond the first paragraph, this book is for you. It is about managing your mind so that your learning, performance and enjoyment of tennis are optimised. It is about how to have the least hassle, the most fun, and how to make the best of the great opportunities junior tennis has to offer.

There are many manuals on the technique of tennis with diagrams of the perfect forehand or the great tactical manoeuvre. There are booklets and articles in tennis magazines that tell you what attitude you should have and what behaviour to adopt on court. All of them are written by top coaches, renowned players or sports psychologists, from the expert's point of view. However, experts are not always so expert when it comes to putting themselves in the shoes or the minds of junior tennis players.

This book is different. It has been collated and ghost-written by a tennis father from the experiences, learnings, jottings and perspective of his son, a junior player who is good at tennis, but by no means the best in his age group. He is striving to get better but he also plays other sports, has other interests and does not have the top of tennis as his only goal. He is a regular teenager with supportive parents and the opportunity to pursue his enthusiasm for tennis. *Mind Games* is written for young players who are embarking on a similar quest, or trying to discover if they want to. Unlike other books by experts, this one adopts the kid's point of view. That kid is me and this is my story so far!

I started playing tennis for fun when I was eight.

My dad said I was quite good – but parents are easily impressed by what their children do. Anyway, because I enjoyed it, he signed me up to play in a tennis squad on Sunday mornings at a local club. I ran around a lot and had fun whacking balls about. When I had learned a bit about how to play properly, I played some short matches against others in the squad. I usually won so I entered a club tournament and won again.

Unexpectedly, and quite suddenly, tennis became more serious. Adults wanted me to do it right and to win. And I wanted to win too. It had been fun beating my dad, but beating other boys who were quite good was another challenge. I began to work at my tennis; sometimes it was hard but it was worth it.

Four years later I won the Twelve and Under, Boys' Singles County Championship, and got a sports scholarship to one of the best tennis schools in England. Representing Sevenoaks School, my partner Will Shaw and I won the 1997 Thomas Bowl, the British Independent Schools Doubles Championship for Boys, Fifteen and Under, and we will still be young enough to play for it again in 1998. In July 1997 I won two out of three of the fourteen and under tournaments entered and quickly accumulated sufficient wins and points to go up two ratings levels in October.

I do not know how far I will get in the future. I have a number of goals along the way, but I take a step at a time. I would like to play seriously (instead of working!) when I finish school, but I know I must be realistic about my chances, and remain open to other choices. Doing well at school will certainly increase the number of choices available to me. Besides, there is more to life than tennis; too much for some!

Because of so many different pulls, many good players give up tennis altogether in their mid or late teens. They seldom regret having been involved, and no one can ever take away what they gained from competing. Even if you do not plan to play serious tennis, I think you will find the ideas in this book will also make a valuable contribution to your other interests and activities.

I intend to stay in tennis and I hope you will too. If so, maybe this book will help you to climb the tennis ladder with more understanding of the journey and more confidence in your ability to reach as high as your dreams. The path to their fulfilment, however, is different for each individual and it can never be predicted, prescribed or guaranteed. I wish you all success in finding your own best way forward.

Jason Whitmore

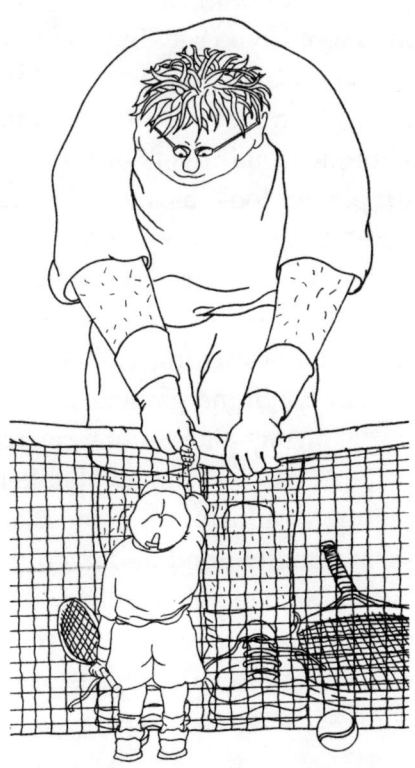

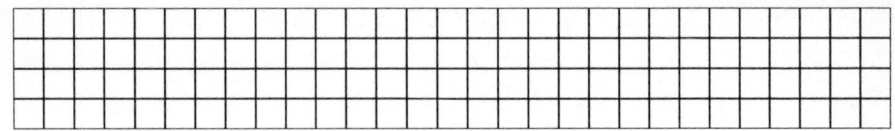

1 Why Play Tennis?

**Tennis is a game of skill and restraint,
and putting the ball where the other guy ain't.**

Attend any major junior tennis tournament and you will be amazed at the high standard of tennis you see. Ten and twelve-year-old girls and boys hit the ball so hard and accurately that they all look like prospective champions. Don't let this put you off, we kids do learn very fast. Their technique, a mini version of the real thing, makes the adult weekend player look as clumsy and unnatural as a drunken chicken trying to fly.

The second thing that may amaze you is how emotional and self-critical many juniors are when they miss a shot or lose a point – more mini McEnroes in the making rather than well-mannered *Henmen*. Tennis is certainly a mind game.

By the time these aspiring players have reached sixteen their performance is awesome; barely distinguishable from what we see at Wimbledon, Flushing Meadows or Roland Garros. To the casual observer they all seem equally good and even the initiated would be unable to pick the winners merely from watching a game or two.

And yet certain players, not necessarily the most spectacular ones, tend to keep reaching the latter stages of tournaments. Even

then, who will actually win on finals day is anyone's guess. So, what are the attributes of a consistent winner at tennis? Natural talent helps, an eye for the ball, so does being tall; strength, fitness and flexibility are important, so is court availability, a good coach and sufficient money to pay for both. Any one of these alone is not indispensable, and all of them together will not make you a winner. Just as it is in most sports, it is what goes on in the player's mind that determines how fast they learn and how far they will go in tennis.

Our relationship with tennis and how well we enjoy, learn and perform will be profoundly influenced by one or more of the following underlying attitudes that are likely to accompany us onto the tennis court:

A. **Low or no motivation.**
B. **Fear of losing or failing.**
C. **Need to win or succeed.**
D. **Desire to improve one's game.**

It would be nice if it were easy to choose which one to adopt. The problem is we are unlikely to be aware of our underlying attitudes or to feel we are able to change them if we are. I suggest that **A** and **B** are unhelpful, that **C** is better, but that **D** is the most healthy attitude and the one that will lead to most wins. At different stages in my brief tennis career, I have been besieged by each of the four attitudes and sometimes possessed a conflicting combination of all of them. I have recently been able to reap the rewards of being driven most of the time by **D**, *the desire to improve*.

For the sake of simplicity we will examine the characteristics and the positive and negative effects of each in order for you to see where you are and to help you to find the best way forward. Let us start with **A**.

Low Motivation

The lack of any real motivation to play hard is difficult to overcome. If you want to play or to play more, harder or better tennis but you can't seem to get it together, there is no instant remedy. However, your motivation will automatically rise if you eliminate those elements that keep it down. First you have to find out what they are.

What is it about tennis that you don't enjoy? You may be able to change it, or at least to ensure you don't repeat the same pattern in your next sport. If you have already invested a lot of yourself in tennis, don't give it up lightly. What drew you to tennis and what was it you liked so much before you lost it? Can you recapture it? If your enthusiasm has died, what or who killed it?

Tennis may not have met your expectations for fun, victory or speed of progress. The physical demands may be higher and harder than you initially expected. The number of dedicated hours required per week to maintain satisfying progress may now be more than you want to give, particularly as you are probably discovering other interests or friends. *Expectations or 'shoulds' are killers.*

We young people derive pleasure from physical expression, exertion and extension beyond what we have achieved before. Does tennis offer this for you? If it does not, maybe you are not *going for it* enough. Some of us find great satisfaction in mastering the challenge of hitting a moving ball to where we want it to go. If doing so holds little excitement for you, then quit. Climbing a rock face or roller-blading may offer you a more satisfying challenge. If you have no desire to compete and winning or losing is unimportant to you, just play for fun or perhaps you should seek a creative or artistic form of expression.

Was it the pressure that others, parents or coaches, put on you to try harder, perform better or improve faster, that you found stressful and which stifled the fun? Unfulfilled expectations and unwanted pressure led me to want to quit more than once. In fact, I did quit for a few weeks. My dad didn't try to make me change my mind; instead, he instantly removed all the pressure. I soon began to play again and to enjoy it. He and I now monitor and manage pressure and expectations more carefully.

If, after identifying and eliminating or reducing the obstacles to your motivation, it still remains low and you decide to quit tennis, you can always pick it up again. The loss of ability even after a break of several months or a year is surprisingly small and if the break renews your enthusiasm, then it will have been no loss at all. On the other hand, if your motivation begins to rise, keep playing but only as much as you want to, no more, no less. What will be, will be!

If you don't enjoy tennis, don't play it.

Life Learning

Whether or not tennis is your sport, do not let the size of the challenge put you off. *There are many life-learning benefits to be had from competing hard in sport, tennis in particular, and they are not dependent on getting even close to the top.* I did not know or care about them when I was nine, and I am only now beginning to realise how many and how great those benefits have already been to me and will continue to be long after I have broken my last string. Just some of the things I have already gained or learned something about are:

- *Self-esteem.*
- *Self-confidence.*
- *Self-respect and respect from others.*
- *Discovering my limits are beyond what I thought possible.*
- *How to cope with pressure.*
- *How to cooperate with others.*
- *How to become intense, effective and focused.*
- *Feeling purposeful.*
- *Getting and staying healthy, strong and physically fit.*
- *Meeting all kinds of friends outside school and home.*
- *Travel opportunities.*

And there will be many more benefits in the future.

Apart from the emotions associated with the ups and downs of competitive tennis, players have to contend with the net, the lines, and the differing skills and character of various opponents, not to mention officials, line judges and umpires. Similarly, in life there will be obstacles to overcome, skills to learn, boundaries to observe, people who will push you to your limits and people with more power and authority than you. It is the same game, just a bigger court. What you learn on the tennis court as a junior is going to make you a better player on the field of life later. Just look at how some adults overreact to what we do on the tennis court, at home or at school. Perhaps they would have benefited from playing a bit more junior tennis when they were young and learning the lessons it offers. And one day we may be parents too!

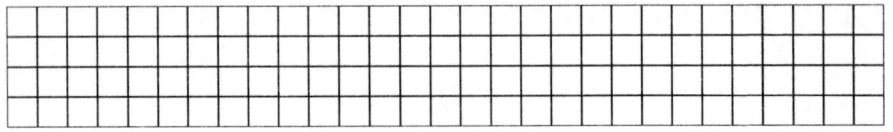

2 **Being Careful**

When we finally give up control
is when we gain it.

Is it how you play the game
or how you place the blame?

The Fear of Losing, or Failing

This is the second underlying attitude that
may inhibit us. Whilst it at least shows some
motivation, it causes us to fall into one or
both of the great traps of junior tennis – being
careful and getting upset with ourselves.

Don't be Careful

How many times did your mother say to you, 'Be
careful,' just before you dropped something? I am
saying to you, *in tennis, don't be careful.*
Trying to be careful will probably cause you
to drop your serve. If you start being
careful in one area of your game,
several other areas may also fall apart.

Why does this happen? When someone says to you, or when you say to yourself, 'Be careful,' it takes your focus of attention away from the ball and on to trying to control the arm that hits the ball. Your arm becomes tense and moves in a stiff and unnatural way. This results in a lousy shot or a miss-hit. Even if you do keep the ball in play, you end up pushing the ball instead of hitting it, the ball, therefore, lands short. Also, since you are being careful not to hit the net or hit the ball out the side of the court, you end up hitting it not only short but high over the net into the middle of the court – a gift to your opponent.

When I was ten I played well in practice but every time I played a match I became too careful. When this happens the most common advice is to play lots of matches and there is no doubt that it does help. My dad, however, took a different approach which felt better to me. He stopped me playing matches altogether for a while and in training got me to hit every ball as hard as I could no matter where it went. Far more of them than I or even my dad expected went where they were supposed to go. From this I learned that being careful was not the only way to get the ball in and going for it hard became my norm in practice and in matches. Although I know this now, I still find myself sometimes slipping back into playing cautiously and have to remind myself to apply what I've learned.

Every summer I play a lot of school doubles matches which are often quite easy. Once, when I was playing the last match of the day, it was a bit tougher than the rest. As I had not been expecting this, I started being careful, pushing the ball and not moving my feet. I wanted not to make any mistakes, but I began making more than ever. I served six double faults and was hitting weak ground strokes which allowed my opponents to hit winners against my partner at the net. This was also happening to my partner and because we were both being careful we were both making mistakes. We did win the match but it was damned hard!

Being careful never helps. It often creates the very problem we are most afraid of. If you are afraid of hitting the net, you are likely to hit the net. Because your focus of attention is on the net, that is exactly where the ball will go. If you are afraid of hitting the ball out, you probably will hit it out. If you are afraid of hitting the ball to your opponent, you will do just that, and *if you are afraid of losing, you will lose!*

The comic strip character Peanuts once said, *'Winning is not everything, but losing isn't anything!'*

It isn't anything on the result card but we can learn a lot from losing, such as: what to do not to lose again; how to handle losing; and, most importantly, that losing is the other side of winning. Just as, if there was no down there would be no up, if there was no losing there would be no winning.

If you are not prepared to lose sometimes, don't play tennis.

Of course, most of us experience little fear of losing when playing better players who we are not expected to beat – older players or players who we have not played before and know little about. However, in certain other situations I still experience my fear of losing and the temptation or tendency to be careful. It usually occurs when I have to play someone who is a good player but who I have always beaten in the past. I am expected to win by myself and by others, *but what if I don't?* Then there is the player in a younger age group who I remember as a mere beginner but who now has a reputation as a rising star. *Can I still beat him?* If I meet my own doubles partner in an out-of-county tournament, we both tend to get nervous and careful though we should be able to use the match as good training.

Trying to talk myself out of my anxiety beforehand often only makes things worse. Getting out on the court and fully focusing on the ball, my own game or my game plan to fill my consciousness with a positive sense of purpose is for me and for most players the best way to sweep aside the caution. And then there is the frustrating unorthodox player with a reputation for having one particular stroke as a very effective weapon. *Will I be able to cope with it?*

Even more frustrating is the hacker.

Hackers

In tennis, hacking means your opponent plays all his or her strokes by defensively pushing the ball back high into the middle of the court, usually quite deep. For them this is a form of being careful; for you it may be a formula for getting upset. They do not try to win the point, but simply wait for you to make a mistake and lose it. This is made more likely by your frustration and your desire to finish off the point, and the opponent, too quickly.

Hacking does not require much tennis technique nor energy, but until players reach about twelve years old the hacker will most often win. Sooner or later their opponent will make a mistake. After twelve, when both power and skill are higher, the hacker will soon be outclassed.

In your early tennis years you may be tempted to become a hacker in order not to lose. While you will win some matches that way, it will not do your tennis or your reputation any good. When you are up against a hacker the trick is to stay calm, take your time

and don't attack the ball until you see the right opportunity. Once you start beating a hacker at their own game, they may decide to stop hacking and start playing proper tennis which will be better for both of you, whoever wins.

Conclusion

The more matches you play, the more you learn that you win some and you lose some. *No one match is important enough to get careful or upset about.* For most of us at first there is a big difference between our practice play and our match play. 'Why can't I play like this in a match?' is a thought we have all had. Well, you can and you will. The sooner you give up being careful and the more matches you play, win or lose, the closer in standard your practice play and your match play will become.

The fear of losing causes us to lose, partly because we become careful and tense and make mistakes; and partly because our thoughts are concentrated on losing and the consequences of losing. So, that is what we do. If, on the other hand, we are driven by wanting to win, our focus will be on winning each point and the match. However, if we are too concerned about winning the match, our thoughts will be on the match instead of on each point and each ball which is where our attention ought to be every time we play.

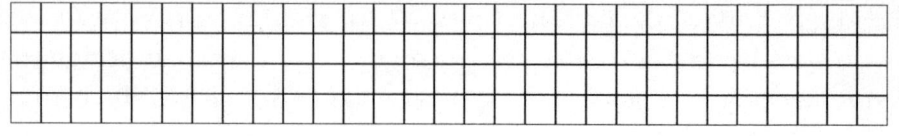

3 **Getting Upset**

The difference between being upset and being set up is all in the mind.

Getting upset with ourselves when we lose a point or a match may be rooted in the *fear of losing* or the *need to win*. Either way, it is the biggest mental problem in junior tennis and most of us experience it at some time. And yet without that tendency, we would not be competitive. It is our search for perfection that makes us strive to do better and to win, and our many moments of imperfection on court that drive us crazy.

Perfectionism, present in abundance in most sports performers is a two-edged sword. All coaches will confirm that they see better prospects in an abusively self-critical player than one who is well behaved but unmotivated and casual about his or her results. Learning to manage, or should I say balance, the advantages and disadvantages of our own particular brand of perfectionism is the skill we must develop.

The Downward Spiral

Missing an easy shot, losing an important point or a bad line call can break our concentration and set us on a downward spiral of frustration and self-criticism. The outward manifestation of swearing and talking negatively about ourselves out loud, or smashing a ball into the netting or the racket onto the ground, not only gives hope and heart to our opponent but may also result in penalties from officials or serious trouble from our parents. The internal effect is that we get tense and lose concentration. Once we have lost that, we are likely to lose the next point, the game and the match as well.

Pre-teen boys and girls may dissolve into tears at the end of a match they have lost or even during a match when things are going against them. While girls tend to stay with tears to express their frustration, most boys will have turned to racket or ball abuse and swearing by the time they are eleven or so – the beginnings of male macho! Both resort to negative-self talk which can be elaborate and even amusing if it was not so self-destructive. I played a boy recently who during both points and between games was saying aloud to himself, 'I didn't want to play this match… I don't want to be here… I am tired… I am hungry – no breakfast… Why don't you quit tennis?… That is the worst shot I have ever seen…' and more. If he was not already losing, he certainly talked himself into it!

It is surprising how early in our tennis career this self-defeat can begin and how far into our teens it may continue. The reaction from tennis officials, our coaches and most parents is simply to demand that we stop doing it and to threaten to ground us. This is singularly unhelpful! Most of us in that state are no longer in control and don't have a clue how to stop doing it. The outward expressions of our frustration do bring us some kind of relief, even if they do nothing for our tennis.

Staying Up or Climbing Back Up

Observing competitors and matches at junior tournaments suggests that the battle is fought more in the mind than on the court. American tennis coach Tim Gallwey wrote in his book, *The Inner Game of Tennis*, that 'the opponent in your head is more daunting than the one on the other side of the net.' Few of us would disagree with this. So what can we do to win the *inner game*?

Ask a small child in mid-tantrum what they are upset about and they are likely to scream at you, 'I am not upset!' Although it is obvious to an outsider that they are upset, they themselves, unbelievably, are unaware of it. So it is with young tennis players. *We can only control that which we are aware of; that which we are unaware of controls us.*

If you can develop the awareness to recognise the first sign in yourself of getting upset, you will be able to keep it under control. It may start with a negative thought, a feeling in your solar plexus, throat or muscles or with an emotion such as anger or resignation. If it creeps up on you unawares, it may be too late and it can take control of you. A method of managing yourself is to rate your upset level on a one-to-ten scale every point or two, with zero representing no upset and ten being as bad as it gets. Monitoring yourself in this way makes you aware of the small beginnings of an upset and, most importantly, causes it to subside which allows your calm focus to return.

Awareness itself is the cure but there is a caution. If, while monitoring yourself in this way, you become critical of yourself for being too high on the scale, you may get upset about being upset with yourself! Then things go from bad to worse. *Only if you rate yourself without criticism, will you see the level of your upset drop.*

Try Using a Ritual

The leading tennis sports psychologist in America, Dr Jim Loehr, studied how the top players who are most successful at managing their emotions behave between points. He noticed a consistent pattern and believed that if he taught others to copy this pattern of behaviour, it would serve them well. He called it the 16-second cure because that is on average the time interval between the end of one point and the beginning of the next serve.

The 16-second cure addresses four different mental states of a player as identified by Loehr. Only one of the states is positive, the other three are negative. He used a diagram to illustrate them.

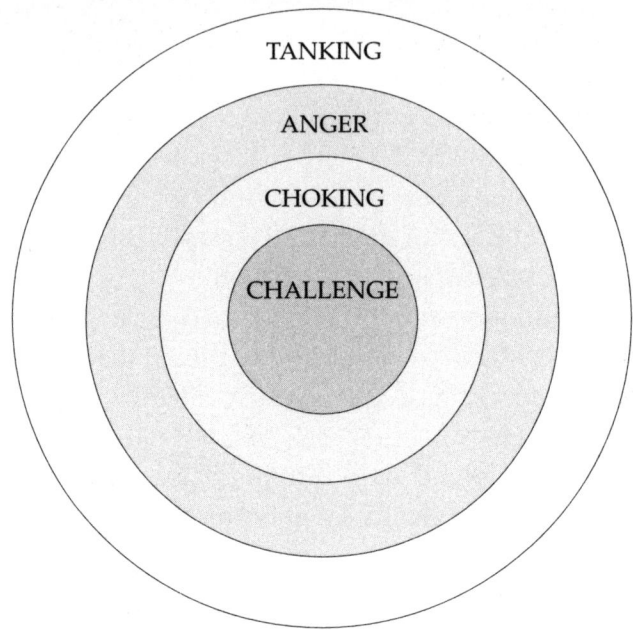

In the Zone. We play our best tennis when our body and mind work in complete harmony. This state is sometimes described as being *in the zone*. It is what we aim for and is at the bull's eye of the target.

Choking is a version of being careful. Usually, it occurs when we are nervous or when we have something to lose. We rush, get tense and are unable to move and think clearly. Our mind and emotions effect the body, and we begin to make mistakes.

Anger. At some time or other, every tennis player has been angry with him–or herself on court, sworn out loud and maybe even thrown down their racket. Sometimes, anger just has to be let out in a shout or some physical action but bad language or bad behaviour leads to penalties and a bad reputation. A quick, managed, release of anger may be necessary before we can get focused and concentrated for the next point. But what happens to our performance if we carry the anger through several points or even a few games? Our tennis goes from bad to worse – we have let anger take control. And anger can lead to tanking.

Tanking is when you give up because you are so annoyed you can't be bothered any more. Tanking is the easy way out of losing. Not caring makes losing easier but, of course, deep down inside we really do care. At least a display of anger shows that you care and are still trying but when you tank you have given up hope. Even when you hit a good shot you give no positive response. You dismiss it as luck or give a disinterested shrug. This is the worst state of all to get into.

The 16-Second Cure

The ideal is to stay *in the zone* and never stray from the bull's eye, and that is what the 16-second cure aims to help you do. It is a between-point ritual that if used all the time simply does not provide the space for negative thoughts and feelings to enter our consciousness. The time between points is divided into four stages of approximately four seconds each.

Stage 1: Positive Physical Response

Pump your fist after a good shot; or express a *come on* combined with a positive body posture even after an error. This means head up, racket head up, too, and shoulders back.

Stage 2: Relaxation

Consciously take a few deep breaths, calm down, and relax. Look or pick at your strings; use them as a focal point as you walk back behind the baseline.

Stage 3: Preparation

Prepare yourself by thinking about your tactics for the next point and what you are going to do (serve 'n' volley or stay back for example). Move up to the baseline, perhaps still looking at your strings.

Stage 4: Rituals

Call out the score and give your opponent a little look as if to say *I am going to win this point*. This is when you bounce the ball before you serve, or jump up and down before you return.

I was lucky enough to have a week of tennis training at Dr Loehr's tennis centre in Florida when I was eleven. Prior to that I used to get

really upset with myself, shout and throw my racket. But when I used the Loehr routine as a ritual, my upsets never even started and I immediately began to play better. I also enjoyed matches more because I did not get so nervous or angry. However, after a few successful weeks I became less disciplined about following the ritual strictly and my frustrations returned.

The 16-second cure definitely worked *if I used it*. But making myself use it all the time was difficult. I used the ritual, it worked, my problem was solved. I imagined it was solved for ever, would stop using the ritual, and the problem would return. I repeatedly watched Loehr's video tape trying to condition myself to do it but it was not until I was fourteen that I managed to really establish it as my own routine. For me, it is not an absolute cure-all. I still occasionally slip, and shout or drop my head for a moment, but I quickly remember to apply the ritual and get back my control which allows my emotional balance to return.

I recently loaned Loehr's tape to two friends who frequently suffered court upsets. He and she and the parents of both now claim that their court behaviour has been transformed by it and their tennis has benefited enormously.

Opponents' Upsets

Remember that your opponents will be subject to all the same upsets as you are but the one who manages these feelings best is the player most likely to win. In a recent tournament final my opponent, who was a year younger than I was but some six inches taller and very talented, started the match with a devastating onslaught. He was attacking every ball and hitting winners hard from anywhere on the court. He was 3–0 up in no time. All I could do was to tell myself to hang in there because he could not, no one could, sustain that level of play. Sure enough, he started to make a few mistakes, began to get upset with himself and he only won two more games in the whole match. Is this not a very familiar tale?

Since so much of tennis is won or lost in our heads, it is reasonable and advisable to take advantage of your opponent's upsets to gain some points or games while their game is down. To do this effectively you need to monitor the signs of your opponent getting upset. This is another very good reason to manage your own external behaviour, whatever turmoil is going on inside, so that your opponent will not be encouraged by your upset. That may be easier said than done unless you use one of the methods just described or another one that works for you.

When you have learned to manage your upsets on the tennis court, you will have learned a skill that will serve you well in all other areas of your life, both now and in the future. It is well worth the effort.

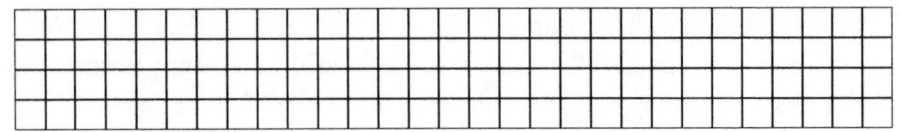

4 Winning, Pressure and Parents

Did your opponent win the match
or did you lose it?

The Need to Win

The majority of children, especially boys, are naturally competitive
and the messages of our society and our parents tend to reinforce
this impulse. We want to win at whatever we do. The shiny plastic
trophies in junior tennis, although materially virtually worthless,
are symbols of our golden achievements. The need to win them is
highly motivating but it has its problems.

We enjoy the recognition and respect we gain from others for our
victories but, perhaps more importantly, they give us self-esteem,
confidence and the courage to set our sights higher next time.
However, if winning comes too easily we may get the recognition
but not the satisfaction of the hard-fought game.

Cheating

Some people are so desperate to win that they will do anything,
including cheat. The trophy they take home may look the same at a

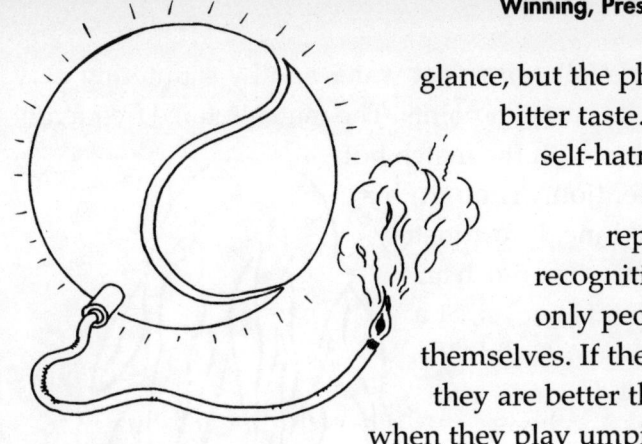

glance, but the phoney glitter has a bitter taste. With it will come self-hatred instead of self-esteem, and a bad reputation instead of recognition. In the end the only people they cheat are themselves. If they begin to believe they are better than they are, later, when they play umpired matches, they quickly learn the painful truth. Inevitably, you will meet a few cheats and you need to know how to deal with them.

If you think your opponent is wrongly calling your balls out, you may challenge a call by asking, 'Are you sure?' If he or she says, 'Yes,' there is nothing you can do about it. If he or she indicates some uncertainty, you may ask them to play the point again. If, in your opinion, your opponent persists in cheating, you may at any time in the match ask for an umpire to be present. Caution: you may get a parent who seems to be blind or who knows little about tennis.

If there is a dispute about the score, you simply go back to the last score you can both definitely agree on and start again from there. If you continue to have scoring disputes you can also call for an umpire but do so only as a last resort. *You do not want to get a reputation as a whinger or as a cheat, or as a player who tries to psyche out their opponent.*

Don't Psyche or be Psyched

On one occasion, I was faced with an opponent who took every opportunity to delay the match with overly-long changeovers, repeated visits to the toilet or to get water and by sauntering very slowly to collect balls between points. The match referee frequently warned him to get on with the match but he paid little attention. Though his behaviour infuriated me, it fortunately did not upset my game too much and I still won the match. However, at a subsequent tournament I did see him cause the breakdown of a far better player than he was.

Some players may be irritating unintentionally. In this case, I suspect the boy had been encouraged to behave in this way by an unscrupulous parent with a win-at-any-price mentality. In one match my opponent's frequent bad line calls were furiously supported by his very aggressive father who also controlled his son from the sidelines throughout the match. This is strictly forbidden. In the end, players and parents such as this defeat only themselves while helping the rest of us to learn how to cope with the unexpected.

The way to cope with it, and with many other of the distractions in junior match play, is to simply focus fully on playing your own game.

Simply focus on playing your own game is in fact the central message of this book but doing so is not always so simple. Although they may not realise it, our own parents can be a major distraction as well as the source of the need and pressure to win.

Winning Versus Improving

For me, pressure really began when I won my first little tournament. It was all such a thrill – to win the last tense point, the relief, the joy, my dad's tearful pleasure, the presentation and my first most treasured little cup.

The pressure came because I then *expected to win* and was also expected to by others. Even if my dad did not expect me to win, I knew that he wanted me to. Winning became important to me to please my dad. He kept telling me that playing my best was more important than winning but I could see his pleasure when I did win. So I tried hard to. But I was making a big mistake by focusing on winning rather than on improving my tennis, learning, or going for it as hard as I could.

Improving your tennis will help you to win, but winning will not necessarily improve your tennis.

Also, if we see success only as coming from winning, we are destined to experience a lot of failure. But if success is learning and improving your game, *then you can succeed every time you play, win or lose.* You have little control over whether you win or not because the other player may be far better than you or be having a very good day and you can't change that. You can control whether you learn or put in your best effort, so when this is your goal *you are in control of your own success.*

It took me a long time to learn that lesson and I will come back to it again in Chapter 5, *Setting Goals*. Before learning it, I was very busy trying to win and being upset when I did not. Of course I didn't always win. However, by the time I was ten I had filled a shelf with cups.

Unfortunately, tennis is very much about winning, unlike the first sport which I took semi-seriously, swimming. In swimming, parents and coaches attach more importance to improving on your previous best time for a certain distance than they do on winning. This seems to be a more productive and less nerve-racking focus. Tennis is just not organised that way.

Parental Pressure

Of course, parental pressure in tennis is not only about winning. They may want us to play more matches or to have more coaching than we want to. They may want us to miss a party because of a match the following day or to train when we want to go to a movie. Probably it would be better for our tennis in the short term if we did these sensible things but, in the long term, if playing tennis causes us to deny too many of our other pleasures we will begin to resent it.

Parental pressure most often stems from love and their wanting the best for us but we do not always experience it that way. It may also come from their desire to bask in the reflected glory of our success, to show us off to their friends and neighbours or to anyone who will listen. Sometimes, they may even unconsciously need us to compensate them for their sporting shortfalls when they were young or even for their current lack of personal achievement. These unhealthy parental pressures may be very strong and persistent and they will often drive us into the very failure our parents most fear.

I have seen parents yell and scream at their children for losing a match they believed the child could have won. I heard a story of a girl whose father pushed her out of their car to run three miles home after she lost a match by, in their opinion, not being fit or fast enough on her feet.

My dad used to get upset with me not for losing but if he thought I was not making sufficient effort in training or in a match. The truth is that it is hard for anyone, especially children, to put in maximum effort all the time. I bet few parents did or even do now but they don't have their parents watching over them! And parents are often less understanding and tolerant of their children's shortcomings than they are of their own. If you do feel unduly pressured by your parents, tell them before it damages your enthusiasm for tennis and ultimately your relationship with them.

On the other hand, our

parents do spend a great deal of time and money enabling us to participate and it is our responsibility to make the best of our talents and their generosity. If we don't want to, then it is only fair to tell them and they can reduce their investment in our tennis accordingly. Some juniors may be too afraid to do so for fear of their parents' anger or the loss of their love, and prefer to continue with tennis rather than confront the issue. That is no solution.

Of course we would not be where we are without adults. I am convinced that they can and do give us more than we ever realise or thank them for. Even the confusing, critical or unhelpful things they do are usually done with the best of intentions. We need to remember they are doing their best – and they need to understand that we are doing our best, too. My mum has been a great support to me and is also a professional psychologist. Here, in her own words, are some recommendations and warnings for other tennis mothers.

Mothers, the Unsung Heroes

It is often the mother who provides the bulk of practical support to an aspiring young tennis player. Fathers are less likely to take time off work to chauffeur their child to training sessions, tournaments and matches. The mother provides this service as well as being the primary source of moral and psychological guidance. A tennis mother needs to be a rock of unconditional support, patience, perseverance and unfaltering acceptance. She needs to make it clear to her child that he or she is valuable and loveable irrespective of the outcome of a match; that his or her well-being is not dependent on results; that winning is not the only or ultimate goal; and that tennis is only a part of life, not life itself.

Most importantly, a mother can help her child understand how tennis is a metaphor for life. I am deeply grateful that through playing junior tennis my son Jason has acquired *life skills* that will benefit him in every aspect of his future. He has learned to motivate himself, set goals and commit himself to those goals. He has learned to contain and regulate his emotional responses under stress. He has learned to win and be gracious. He has learned to lose but not lose self-respect. He has learned that it is his being that matters most, not what he does or achieves. He has learned to channel his energies towards constructive endeavour. I consider these to be the true gifts of all junior competitive sport.

Tips for Tennis Mothers

Unless we are tennis experts of some kind, our task is not to try to improve our child's tennis. It is more important for us to be a source of unconditional positive regard and to see our child as a valuable and worthwhile person simply because he or she exists. Our child's overall well-being is our primary concern. We do not want our child to experience pain, but if we know they suffer when they lose we may unconsciously develop an *attachment to their results*. We must therefore remain alert to the possibility that we may be subtly communicating to our child that it is not OK if they perform poorly or lose a match. We should avoid doing so.

Focus on the Positive

A child will tend to focus their attention, especially when they lose a match, on what they did wrong, how badly they played, etc. This tends to undermine their confidence and self-esteem. The situation can easily be redeemed by helping your child to shift their awareness to what they did well and by asking them what they can learn from the experience. In this way a loss or poor performance can be turned into a creative learning opportunity. However, when a child first comes off court, win or lose, experience has shown me that it is best to give them space and time before talking about it. Often feelings and emotions about the match or training session are too raw and undifferentiated to be processed immediately.

Young Players Seek Perfection

Tennis has always seemed such a lonely sport to me. When I see my child out there on court, all alone, facing the challenge of competition, I am staggered by the implicit drive and thrust towards perfectionism that I perceive. Of course, many will say that it is this perfectionism that drives a player to succeed and that it should not be quelled. I agree, but it should be tempered, otherwise self-criticism will run riot.

If a child is a perfectionist with their tennis, they are also likely to be so in other areas of their life. Tennis provides a good opportunity for the child to *learn to manage their drive for perfection*. I have often noticed that, regardless of the result, a child will not feel good about it if they did not perform to the standard they expect of themselves. There may well be a gap between how they envision themselves playing and how they actually play. Learning to close this gap is an important lesson that will apply to all areas of your child's life and you would do well to help them understand this.

How can you do that? Probably, only you who know your child so intimately can have an answer to this. Each child is unique, so there can be no sure-fire method to follow. The best answer is for the mother to take the child's feelings seriously. Do not try to talk them out of the vision they have of how they expect themselves to play. That vision is a powerfully motivating force. However, help them to understand there may be a gap between their vision and performance and that it is OK if they don't immediately fulfil their own expectations.

Variation in Performance

There is a tendency for a girl's performance to be lower when she is menstruating. Top-level, female, junior tennis players consistently report that their performance goes down noticeably during days of pre-menstrual tension (PMT) and menstruation and they dread big matches that coincide with these periods. Encourage your daughter to accept that her performance on these few days *may* be lower and to remember that her full power and energy will soon be surging back into her.

You're OK!

Many tennis kids simply want their mother to *be there* on the side of the court beaming encouragement and support – with a thumbs-up sign, a nod or wink, or with any other gesture that means, 'I believe in you. You're OK. You can do it.' No kid wants their mother to frown and shake her head in recrimination in a way that not so subtly implies, 'you should do, or be better'.

Your Reward

Finally, don't expect appreciation or acknowledgement for all you do and the time you dedicate to your child's tennis career. Competitive junior tennis is as mentally exhausting for the mother as for the young player. At the end of a full day supporting your child through a tournament, you may get home so mentally drained that you will be unable to do anything remotely constructive.

Your presence and steadfastness will almost inevitably be taken for granted. But to provide the opportunity for your child to enter into competitive sport is both a privilege for you and a gift to your child. It provides perhaps the healthiest opportunity for your child's interaction with a wider society and will serve them well for the rest of their life. You are investing in their long term development.

You May Not Always Get it Right

You may not always be able to manage your own emotions appropriately; and you may, at times, let your child down and feel guilty about it. You will want their opponent to double fault on match point; you will feel their opponent's line calling is not what it might be; and you will feel critical of your child's play. You may forget the sandwiches or put the wrong filling in them. And what about the spare shirt, socks, sweater, water bottle, and headache pills – for your child and yourself? At moments, you may feel you are failing as a mother but hang in there, we all get it wrong sometimes *and*, in the long term, your career as a tennis slave will have served your child immeasurably!

THANKS MUM!

See, I remembered this time!

Diana Whitmore is from California, was trained in psychosynthesis in Italy, and now chairs an educational charity in London which provides university degree training for counsellors and psychotherapists. She is the author of two books, *Psychosynthesis and Education* and *Psychosynthesis Counselling in Action*.

Parental Support

I reproduce here a note my dad left on my breakfast table before a tournament he was unable to attend. It summarises the message of this book and indicates how parents can best support us.

Dear Jason,

Today you may not win the outer game, the match, or the tournament. Doing so is not totally in your control for you cannot control how your opponent plays. On the other hand, you can win the inner game, the game with your own mind. That is totally within your control.

If you win the outer game you will win a cup or two, some rating points and some praise. In a month, that will be forgotten. Everyone, including you, will have moved on to another match, another tournament.

But if you win the inner game, if you manage yourself, your preparation, your attitude, and your intensity throughout the tournament, without a glitch, you will have won far more. You will have won a vital game in the tournament of life.

The prize is self-reliance, self-esteem, confidence, self-respect and the sheer joy of knowing you can master your mind. These things will be with you and support you for your whole life, long after the cups are tarnished or lost.

I have great and unfailing faith in your ability to win the inner game. You have demonstrated that at times, especially recently. Now is the time to win it all the time.

Dad.

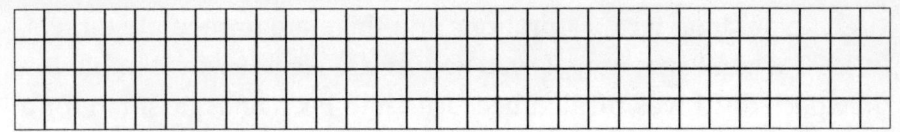

5 Setting Goals

Things happen because we make them happen, not just because we want them to.

Of course it feels great to win. We all want to, but the way to win is to *improve our game*. One of the most valuable elements of the strategy to improve is to set targets for ourselves. There are basically two kinds of goals and they effect our performance in different ways. Hitting 50 forehands non-stop into a marked area, speeding up footwork, or getting 60% of first serves in are what we call *performance goals*. Our achievement of them, or failure, is absolutely within our control. *Your performance is totally up to you.*

Winning certain matches or getting into certain squads, which depend on factors outside our absolute control, are end goals. You cannot control how good your opponent is or how good are the other players are who are vying for the place on the squad. We and our coaches will have more success if we work on those things we do have control over, not those we don't. *Of course we will have some end goals but the way we will best achieve them is by focusing on our performance goals.* The importance and value of striving for better performance rather than for winning has already been pointed out in Chapter 4.

There are long term aspirations and there are immediate targets. In 1992 when I was nine, I watched Andre Agassi win Wimbledon unexpectedly. I was thrilled because I had been an Agassi fan for a couple of years. Jeremy Bates had equally unexpectedly reached the quarter finals and the commentator remarked that a Brit had not won the Wimbledon men's title since Fred Perry in 1936. I said to myself that day, 'Wouldn't it be great to be the next Brit to win.' The idea inspired me to work harder in my squad for a month or two. It was my goal, or so I thought at the time.

I was very innocent then. I had no idea how much work has to be put into getting to the top of anything, and how many thousands of people are trying to do the same thing. I thought a bit of natural talent, which I was told I had, a good racket, and going to the squad each week would get me there. Had I known more at the time, I might not have persevered with tennis – except that I *was* having fun.

The reality is that the route to the top of tennis is like climbing Mount Everest, the highest mountain in the world, and about the same number of people reach the summit. There are millions of steps, large and small, that have to be taken. The early steps in the foothills are easy but the higher you get the tougher it is and the easier it is to fall. Some planning is necessary for a walk in the foothills, but to go any higher, thorough planning is vital if you are to survive and get to the top.

Dreams Inspire Us To Go For It

However, back to now and to tennis. Sooner or later some adults will start going on at you about your goals and plans for achieving them. My first reaction was that I did not want to know, I just wanted to have fun. Adults wanted me to have goals, I didn't. I just wanted to win Wimbledon! So I did have a goal after all. I soon realised that winning Wimbledon might be a very pleasant dream, an inspiration, an aspiration, but it could not be a goal – not yet anyway!

Goals also inspire us by presenting challenges that we strive to meet in order to experience the pleasure of success. If we are not stretched by our goals, they do not help us to improve and there is no gain. On the other hand, goals need to be realistic. If they are too difficult, we will become discouraged and give up. *A useful goal will lie between being too easy to be of interest and unattainable. And our goals will change as we progress.* But here comes the problem: *what adults think are good goals and what inspires us may be two different things.*

Early Goals

Our early intention is probably just to have fun, but that was never really a goal for me because I had fun anyway. *Playing well* was not a goal either. I did not know enough about tennis to really know what *playing well* was. I just knew about playing. Playing well was an adult expression and it was judged by their criteria, not mine.

Hitting lots of balls around always pleased me. However, when I hit them hard and they landed in the court, it seemed to please adults as well. Then there were other things that pleased them, like moving my feet a lot, so I tried to do that too. My intention, in part, shifted to trying to please adults. I was, of course, now attempting to meet their goals, not just my own.

Short Term Performance Goals

We soon begin to set ourselves little goals, like getting the ball over the net ten times, winning the next point – or, in my case, beating my dad. But Dad also set me a goal by saying, 'See if you can beat me this time.' He also set me little goals about learning, 'Try to get six serves in a row in.' I still set myself many little short term goals, such as 25 cross-court forehands without a mistake; to hit all my ground strokes beyond the service line; or to maintain high intensity throughout a lesson (see Chapter 6).

I find when I choose a goal for myself in a squad, it works better than when the coach tells me to do something. It helps me more if he asks me what are my goals for this lesson, this squad, this match or even this game. It reminds me that I have a purpose for being there, without imposing his goal on me. I get to choose my own.

Intermediate Term Performance Goals

Of course the best coaches do encourage simple short term goal setting but they also bring to squads and lessons goal sheets for us to fill in, or they do it with us. These have spaces for match goals, fitness goals, technical goals, tactical goals and mental skill goals. Most coaches will ask what your goals are and will tell you what they think they ought to be, what you are going to learn this month, what fitness drills you are expected to do, how often and with what time improvement, and the like.

The reason and the value of having all these different goals is to give focus and direction to our learning, and intermediate goals do work for me. While I have suggested it is more motivating to go for goals which we set for ourselves, it is also true that we often do not know what goals we should be going for and may need advice from our coach.

Long Term Performance Goals

In reality, however, most of us only fill in the long term goal sheets to keep the coaches and our parents happy, and we don't get many of the benefits of them. Coaches continue to produce them in hope but with little expectation. Maybe it will change soon, but I am still at the stage where tennis paperwork seems too much like school homework and that tends to put me off. I doubt if the benefits of goal sheets offset the negative effects they have, and most other young tennis players feel the same way.

The fact that these goals are at least partially imposed on us and we are obliged to keep working on them, inhibits the short term goal setting that we do instinctively. Besides, I don't think long term goals are especially helpful until we are a bit older. Adults may think in terms of next summer or next year, but our thinking is more immediate. I think we should be allowed to come to serious goal setting later, when we are ready to. If you remain unconvinced about the value of some goal setting and the value of improving over winning, consider this:

If winning is the most important thing to you, I can offer you a tip that will guarantee you never lose another tennis match in your whole life. Do you want it? Think how it would be if every time you played a match you knew you were going to win. I bet you would soon get bored and give up tennis.

If you still want the tip, send me a copy of the best action photo you have of yourself playing tennis and write one paragraph describing what you enjoyed most about your best match win.

Don't forget to include a stamped, self-addressed envelope. By return post you will receive a method of ensuring you never again lose a match. Write to:

Jason Whitmore, c/o Element Children's Books, The Old School House, The Courtyard, Bell Street, Shaftesbury, Dorset SP7 8BP, United Kingdom.

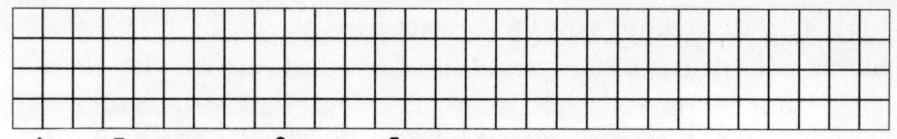

6 Intensity, Awareness and Honesty

Intensity is perhaps the greatest attribute a tennis player can have.

Nothing will improve your game more than learning, training and playing with high intensity at all times; followed closely by being aware and honest with yourself.

One day, I had played three matches and completed a one hour lesson with my individual coach. I was knackered, but I still had another hour to go with an assistant coach. I was playing all right but with very low intensity and looking as if I didn't want to be there. The problem was that I didn't recognise it. The coach suddenly said to me, 'Either play with intensity or don't play at all.' He asked me how intense I was on a scale of 1–10. I said I was about 8, but his estimate was 4. Then he got me to observe and rate my intensity level while I was playing. My intensity quickly rose from 4, which I realised had been about right, to 9 and I played much better despite being tired.

It is vital to play with intensity. If you are tired, it is better not to play or to play really intensely for half your time on court and then stop. Stretching yourself for a short time will not do any harm and may help to prepare you for five-set matches in the future. Your tennis will benefit more from a short burst of intense play than it will if you continue to practise because you think you should and play your whole lesson with a low intensity.

In match play, intensity does not begin at the start of the first point; it should begin way before. Your warm-up and knock-up are well understood to be for physical preparation, but they are also key for your mental preparation. Do both with high intensity and you will start your match explosively and blow your opponent away!

How to Increase Intensity

Increasing and maintaining motivation, or intensity, at all times when playing is the next challenge. To some extent, it still is for me. When there is no real pressure to make me nervous and when I really want to win, as I do when I play points with my coach, my feet fly. But when I am in a rather flat squad or playing an easy match, I have to make a real effort to play with intensity.

You might ask, 'Why should I play intensely if I can get the result without?' The fact is that along with intensity comes a focus on the ball, a bending of the knees, a forward posture, and an explosiveness in the body that almost guarantees perfect timing and accuracy. When you are not so intense, what you are actually doing is practising less than top quality timing, knee bending, racket-head speed and the rest. You are building that into your physical experience, into the store from which you will draw your shots in future.

You are practising the wrong thing when you are not intense.

It was at Nick Bolletieri's Tennis Academy in Florida that I had the most intense experience of practising and playing continuously with intensity. The atmosphere of the whole place is so charged with activity, enthusiasm, high energy and high tennis standards that even the most lethargic player is liable to become infected. The coaches are tough and they push you but always with fun and humour. Music often blares across the courts and Nick darts from one court to another giving staccato instructions and tips with disarming effect. Not infrequently, a top ATP player is practising on the court next to you and even the juniors have world rankings. It is hard not to be intense there even at seven in the morning and often for hours on end, and it is hard not to play well when you are so intense.

For me, fast footwork comes from intensity, but where do I get intensity from when I am not surrounded by it? Sometimes, it just comes naturally and that is fine but I want to learn how to turn it on at will, to bring it under my control. Being told or telling myself to be intense doesn't work. It is rather like telling someone to relax when they are tense. They know they need to relax but the command doesn't help. In fact, it probably makes them more tense.

I have often thought I was playing with intensity and moving well, yet the result and feedback from others indicated that I was not. So, what is a strategy to increase intensity?

Only quite recently I became aware for the first time while on court that I was not playing with intensity. As soon as I noticed it, I became more intense. It made me realise that I have to notice for myself any flaws in my game before I can eliminate them. In fact, they tend to eliminate themselves as soon as I notice them. It is sometimes hard to accept criticism or even feedback from other people, but . . .

When you notice something for yourself, there can be no denial.

Whenever you play, keep a mental check on your level of intensity and rate it on a scale of 1–10 every couple of points. When I monitor my intensity in this way I find it gets higher and higher – without effort or self-criticism.

The more aware you become of your level of intensity, the higher it will become.

Maintaining a high level of intensity is such a complete and focused state that it does not leave space for self-critical thoughts and the upsets that follow them.

How to Learn Other Things

The principle of mental and emotional self-awareness that helps me to build my intensity or reduce my upset can also be applied to the body and to improving technique. If someone tells me to drop the racket head before a forehand, I may do so for the next two strokes, then I revert to doing it as I always have. But if I monitor how much my racket head is dropping before I hit the ball, it begins to drop all the time.

Non-judgmental awareness of your own experience of your mental state or your physical movement as it is happening is more valuable to you than subsequent observations from another person irrespective of how expert they are. Awareness is sometimes called the *here and now*, as opposed to the *there and then* of feedback from others which describes the past, or feed-forward which is intended to influence the future. Awareness should not be confused with analysis or assumption. However, its usefulness will be dependent on how self-aware you are able to be with yourself. Understanding the full effect of awareness and how to become more aware is addressed further in Chapters 9 and 10, but let us look at honesty here.

Honesty

Read again the little story in the first paragraph of this chapter. Was I just unaware that my intensity level was low, or was I kidding myself when I first rated my intensity as 8? A degree of both, I think. I gave the number I wanted it to be rather than the one it was. I gave my coach the number I thought he wanted to hear rather than the one it was. As long as I maintained my belief that it was an 8, not much improvement was available. When I admitted that it was only a 4, considerable improvement was available, and I could do something about it.

Lack of honesty with ourselves, or with our coach, inhibits change.

To be honest with ourselves, we need to be free of fear, the fear that is generated by criticism from others or from ourselves. That sort of fear is sometimes instilled in us at a very early age by the threatening behaviour of our parents or school teachers; but, whatever its source, now is the time to let go of it. Perhaps we are afraid of the truth because it is liable to make us feel bad about ourselves. We prefer to live in the comfort of a positive fantasy. That is fine if emotional comfort is what you want, but it is not fine if you want to get better at tennis or at handling the mental states involved in tennis – or in anything else.

Use the 1–10 scale for assessing your mental, emotional or physical experience but be as honest as you can with yourself and your coach. If you are not sure of the rating, play a few more strokes or points, monitoring it carefully before you answer. Attempting to be honest will cause you to raise your awareness to higher and higher levels. When you do this, not only does your performance improve but your speed of learning and your enjoyment also increases.

Criticism, from yourself or others, reduces awareness; your own honesty increases it.

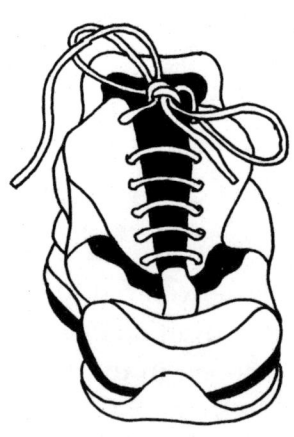

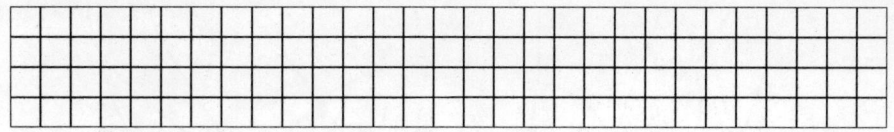

7 Expectation and Preparation

Ready for every ball, ready for life.

Improving Your Game

To improve your game you must be both physically and mentally prepared to learn, to train and to play. Intensity, honesty and awareness are mental requirements. Managing expectations is another, and there are a number of short and long term physical requirements for every junior tennis player.

Expectations

Expectations of all kinds, both positive and negative, as well as the unexpected, can cause us problems. What we need to have is no expectations, which is not the same as the unexpected. Being hit by the unexpected means that we had expectations of something different and usually better. We were unprepared for what happened. If we have no expectations it means we are equally prepared for whatever may happen and are better equipped to cope with anything that does. And anything can and does happen in junior tennis.

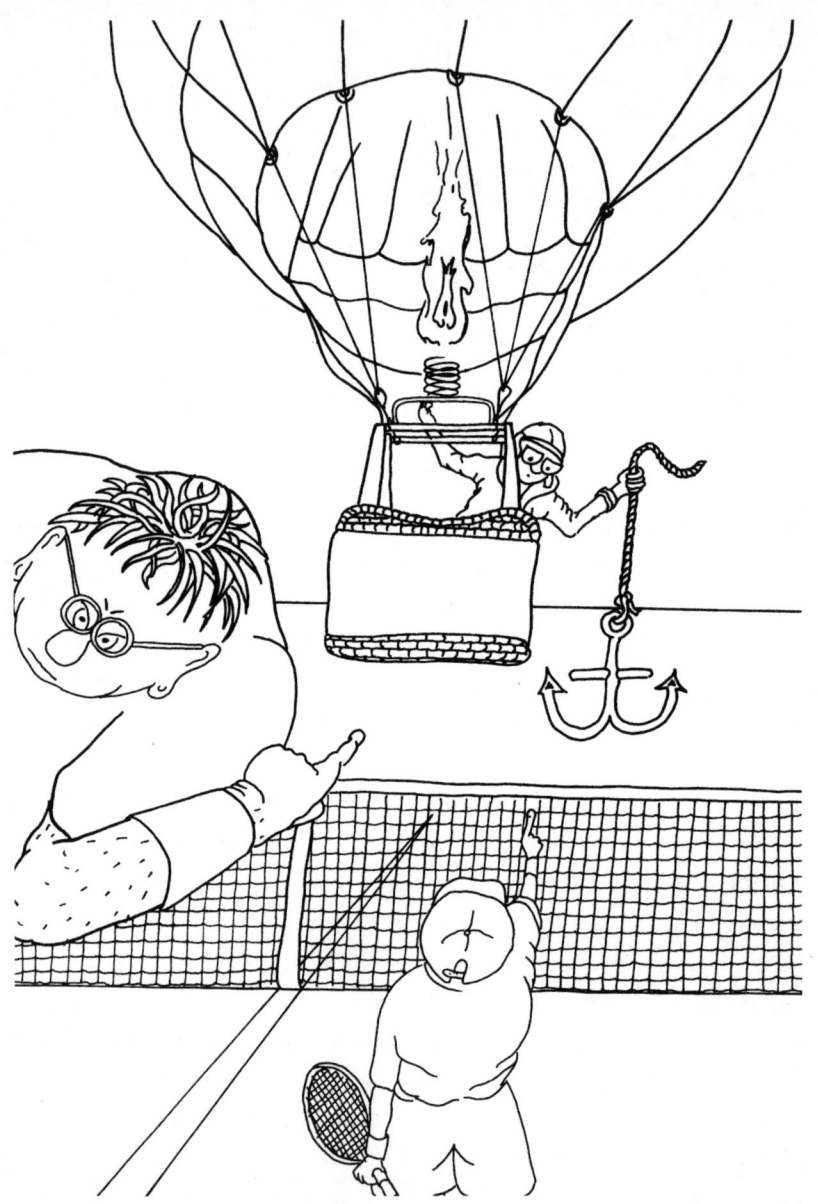

Positive Expectations

Positive expectations need to be realistic. If they are overly optimistic we will be disappointed when we fail to fulfil the expectation. This not only applies to matches but to training as well. One time with my coach, I had six consecutive really good lessons in which I played *in the zone* (see page 30). When I subsequently had a lesson that was not bad but was more my normal standard of play, I got upset because I had built up such a high expectation of myself in my lessons. I was putting pressure on myself to play amazingly again, instead of taking it as it came, and was therefore unnecessarily disappointed.

Negative Expectations

Negative expectations don't help either, because instead of being pleasantly surprised when you do better than expected, you tend to get what you expect. For example, if you repeatedly miss a certain shot in practice or a match and you are forced to play it again, you tend to immediately think about the ones you have already missed. In your mind's eye you see yourself missing the shot again, and what happens? Of course you miss the shot, or you look to see *if* you have missed it before you have finished the stroke. This causes you to miss it anyway.

Ups and Downs

In a game or a match you may experience several minor ups and downs. You will learn that losing the first set is not a disaster and that winning the first set is no guarantee of winning the match. Whatever the odds, it is the ability to keep playing your game consistently right up to the last point that leads to success.

Don't let the downs get you down!

The same holds true for much longer time scales. The path of a person's tennis development is never a continuous steady incline. The yardstick we tend to use, though it is not the best, is how we are performing compared to our peers. If we look at those who began at the same time we did or who were in the same squad as us and compare our current performance to theirs, we will at times be elated and at times be deflated. Those ups and downs in our relative performance may last for six months or more.

Don't let the long-term downs get you down either!

I fell behind my peers for some eighteen months, a period that included four months off with injury, but it could not be accounted for only by that. For a while I struggled with my motivation and my inability to master certain things my coach was working on with me. I did not want to play matches for fear of failure and when I did, not surprisingly, my results were mediocre. I dropped below my peers in the ratings. I even considered giving up tennis.

However, something kept me going. Perhaps it was my stubbornness combined with the flashes of near brilliance that I produced every now and again when playing points against my coach. I dreamed of stringing the flashes together in a real match. John Shepherd, my coach, and my dad seemed to have more faith in my potential than I did, and they kept encouraging me.

Then, all of a sudden in July 1997, it all seemed to come together. Every match I played seemed better than the last. Within a two-week period I won two tournaments in singles and one in doubles, beat five players two rating levels above me, and earned over one thousand rating points at one tournament alone. Accolades and cups followed and the expectation of a double jump in my rating. I was back in the system and in my place with a vengeance. The smell of success was sweet, I was on a high.

I am fully aware that highs are by their very nature inevitably preludes to lows. I will fight long and hard to prolong the high, but I need to be realistic now, and resilient when darkness comes. At sometime, my story will be a familiar one to you; maybe it already is. But always remember that day always follows night!

None of this should surprise us. We all have differing ways and rates of learning and consolidating different things, and there is much to be learned in tennis. Our time of tennis development coincides with a powerful stage in our physical, mental and emotional development. There will be periods when these forces are all at odds with one another, and there will be others when they coalesce in a powerful forward thrust. We need to learn to manage the effects of both.

The Unexpected

When I was thirteen I was playing a final against an out of county opponent. It was a tough match and he led 5–4 in the first set. When I won the next game to even the match, my opponent started crying and ran to embrace his mother beside the court. I did not know what to do. There was no umpire present. It was at least ten minutes before he came back on the court and we began to play again, with him still crying. When I won the next three games and therefore the set, he again ran to his mother.

They left the building for nearly twenty minutes while I lost my warm-up, my focus and my motivation. I should then have demanded that he concede the match. However, I didn't and he returned once more still in tears. I took the first two games of the

second set and he ran from the court again. By that time an official had returned and the boy was obliged to concede. The whole incident was quite unnerving, but a useful lesson in being prepared for anything. *If this sort of thing happens to you, keep moving and focus on your movement, or even close your eyes and focus on your breathing for a while. Don't get caught up in the drama.* Another more common example of distraction is when you really want to play and are feeling well prepared both mentally and physically, and you are told at the last minute you cannot play because the match is postponed. This can really get you down. By the time you're on court an hour or so later, you may have lost your will to play. You do not warm up with the same enthusiasm as before. The spring has gone from your feet and it's very hard to get it back. You may even feel you cannot be bothered to play.

A low often feels lower after being on a high. Unutilised adrenaline in your system makes you feel tired. This even happened to me once when I was really pumped up for a lesson with my coach. There was a double booking and I had to wait an hour before playing. By the time the other player's lesson was over, I did not want to play. I could not play with any intensity. I felt I had no energy. I did not play well and got upset with myself. *Rather than wait around being irritated, I should have gone for a walk or a run, and only come back in time for my normal preparation.*

DO YOU PLAY TENNIS TO GET FIT, OR GET FIT TO PLAY TENNIS?

Physical Pressures

Injuries are not caused by lack of physical preparation, but physical preparation of all kinds offers you the best protection against injury, the possibility of which is ever present when we push ourselves physically. As you get older, get higher up in tennis, and your expectations rise, the demand for optimal physical training for court speed, strength and fitness increases and that is not nearly as much fun as hitting tennis balls. In fact, for most of us it is a real drag and we do everything we can to avoid it even when we know it would help our tennis. For some players this is a very hard one to overcome. I hate running unless I have a ball to chase. I hated school athletics and, what's worse, I was often in the last three of any race.

Then there is the other side of the same coin. Too much tennis or exercise with insufficient recovery and body rest time can lead to overuse and injury in a young developing body, especially during

growth spurts. Our own body will protest but often we feel the signs too late and monitoring by parents and coaches or even a physiotherapist is no bad thing.

Speed

It is sometimes said that *a coach can make a player run, but only the player can make themselves run fast*. Of course, what we need is physical strength and practice but most importantly we need the desire to be fast. I used to have a real problem with court speed. My coaches and my dad were always on at me about it. They forced me to do what are known as *court sprints*. These consist of running between and touching court lines or picking up strategically placed balls one at a time in a specified sequence, and putting them in a pile behind the base line.

We would have to do them forwards, backwards and sideways using small steps and sometimes *crossovers*. We would do them against each other, against a stopwatch, as a punishment for not moving fast enough on court, or for any other misdemeanour. I was supposed to do them at home, before school, before the squad, and in the holidays. I avoided doing them in every way I could.

I still dislike that kind of training but, even though I am not very tall and I have huge feet, I am now seen by coaches and even my dad as being fast on court. I discovered my ability to move fast in one particular match against an older and better player. I had nothing to lose, I was feeling great and went for it like hell. I didn't notice what was happening but after the match everyone commented on how well and how fast I had moved.

The cat was out of the bag, I *could* do it. I could no longer pretend to myself or others that I could not physically do it. I am not offering this as an excuse for not doing vital physical training, but I believe that our speed on court depends more on our motivation on the day than on the amount of court sprints we may have done recently. *In other words your court speed lies in your head as much as in your feet.*

Height

Size is supposed to be an advantage in tennis. The taller you are, the longer your reach, the longer your stride, the harder you serve and the higher you serve from. In our early teens we all tend to go through a growth spurt, but for some it starts later than others. It is not unusual to play against someone the same age who is a foot shorter than you are or, as in my case, a foot taller. Those of us who are short are forced to make up for our size with our speed.

As a junior if you lack height or grow late, you are of course vulnerable to being lobbed. To avoid being beaten in this way you will be tempted to stay back and play from the baseline. You will win more matches now this way, perhaps, but are you playing for now or for your future? We learn technique fastest when we are younger, and if you want the serve and volley to be an important part of your game in the future, it is best to use it now. I am still quite short, but I like to serve and volley so I expect it to be one of my weapons in the future. I lose a few points now by being lobbed, but my serve and volley are coming on well.

So much for the future and the expectation of growing, but what if we don't grow? Michael Chang is only 5 foot 9 inches and he has been one of the top ten players in the world for longer than any other player. Andre Agassi and Thomas Muster, at 5 foot 11 inches, were both number one in the world. They are exceptions, and it is

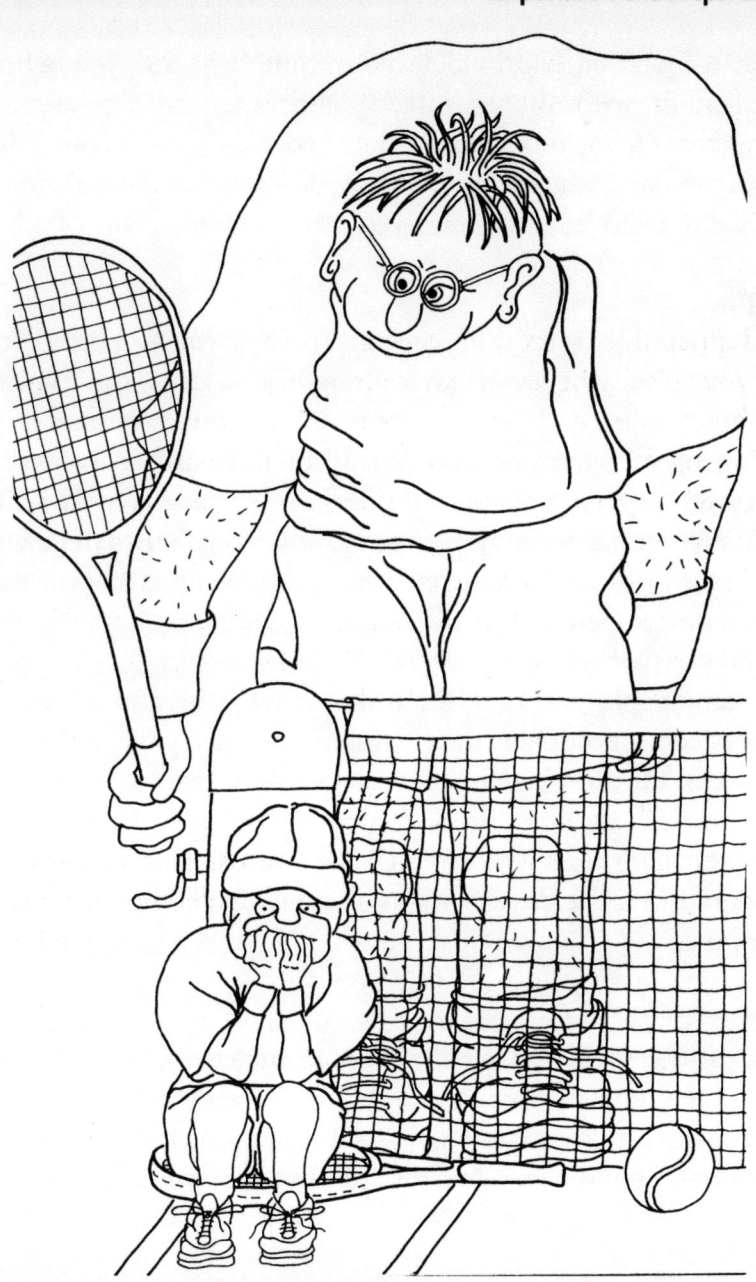

said that 6 foot 1 inch provides the optimum height, stride and reach together with the required agility, mobility and speed. Knowing that being relatively undersized was good enough for Chang, Agassi and Muster should provide enough encouragement for the rest of us to stay in tennis. What about strength?

Strength

Physical strength is important because it helps you to hit the ball really hard. Also, when you have strength in reserve you are less likely to get injured. However, both hitting the ball hard and remaining injury free are as much to do with flexibility and physical efficiency as they are with sheer strength. It is possible to build strength and improve your flexibility and body efficiency with muscle building and stretching exercises. The reality is that most of us are just not prepared to do them and we end up making the best use of the way we are.

Most tennis players find their dominant arm and shoulder muscles become noticeably larger than the other side and some muscle work on the passive side may be desirable to restore the balance. Aside from that, the bodies of most tennis players retain reasonable proportions, and competitive tennis is known to be an excellent sport for the development of the whole body and for all-round fitness.

Fitness

Stamina or the fitness to play a three hour match without flagging is again something that some people are more blessed with than others. Fitness can be improved a lot by continuous and repetitive exercise, like running, but most of us find that very boring and often manage to find something more important to do.

A good excuse, but one which contains some truth, is that distance running can actually slow down your sprint speed. There is, however, really no excuse for not doing sprint drills. I should know for I have looked everywhere for one!

Skipping is an excellent brief exercise which can be done anywhere everyday. It is very good for developing and strengthening the foot muscles and tendons which are so important for the fast starts and direction changes that are essential in tennis. Even if you have never skipped before it does not take long to learn and playing with all the variations of skipping is a challenge and fun to master.

Warm Up

Independent of any long-term physical improvement regimes, it is essential every single time before we play to spend ten minutes or more stretching, skipping and running forwards, backwards and sideways around a court. If we do not, we are liable to get muscle or tendon injuries which can put us out of tennis for weeks.

When you first started playing tennis, the coach probably made you run round the court and stretch before your squad or your individual lesson began. You probably did it because you had to, not because you wanted to, and therefore put as little effort into it as you could get away with. At least, if you are anything like I was, that is what you did. That minimal action will do nothing to either loosen you up or protect you from injury. It is a ritual without value.

The only truly useful warm-ups and stretching occurs when you do it purposefully for your own good. The most effective way is to go through the warm-up routine you have been taught, all the time

focusing your attention on feeling the part of the body in use and extending the stride or stretch towards its natural threshold just within the comfort range. Stretches should not be forced or bounced but held until the releasing is felt, and then extended again. Dynamic warm-ups should continue until you and your muscles are actually warm and loose. This may require more time and attention given to certain areas and movements than others and will be determined by your feeling experience on the day.

Quite apart from protecting yourself from injury, warm-ups will effect your standard of play. If you do not do them before a match, you are likely to start the match slow and tight physically, your timing will be off and your intensity will be low. You can easily lose three games before you wake up and get moving. Even though this message is frequently repeated by coaches and parents, junior tennis players often try to avoid doing a proper warm-up and it is at considerable cost to themselves and their results.

Knock up

Before any match you will have about five minutes to knock up with your opponent. You should have already warmed up, and had a practice hit with a friend or even against a wall; this time should be spent getting your feet moving fast and your timing right. The knock-up should be carried out with the same intensity that you want to apply to the match itself. This will enable you to start fast and take three games off your opponent before he/she wakes up and gets moving. Unfortunately, few juniors ever knock up with sufficient focus and intensity to start as well as they could.

Disappointment

Even with all the preparation and especially without it, accidents, illnesses and injuries can and do happen to any of us. When it does happen and you are told that you will not be able to play for several months, it may at first be a devastating shock and disappointment. You may feel that your peers will all leave you behind, you will never be able to catch them up again and effectively your tennis is over. It is not.

It happened to me. I had a unique opportunity to be at Nick Bollettieri's Tennis Academy in Florida for six months when I was just thirteen. Six months with no school and seven hours tennis a day seemed like heaven. I was having a wonderful time, getting on really well, playing great tennis for three months – and then it happened. I tore a tendon in my foot and had to stop immediately. The treatment was at least three months with no tennis at all, and even then it would be a slow and gentle return.

I left Bollettieri's knowing that an opportunity of a lifetime had come to a premature end. It was a hard pill to swallow but swallow it I did, and four months later I began playing again in England. It took me a while but I am now back on track again and can see that the break may have made me more determined. Another friend of mine had to have an operation on his foot and was out for six months, but a year later he too recovered his place. If it happens to you, and I hope it does not, don't give up. You will be back before you know it. Two years on, the incident will be but a distant memory.

Parental Example

Your parents, as well as your coaches, may try to get you to perform your physical preparation responsibly. If your parents are unfit and overweight, you may think this is unjust or use it as an excuse for not doing what you need to do. But who are you doing it for, them or yourself? If you are doing it for yourself, you should have no concern about what your parents do or don't do. Having said that, there is nothing better than a good parental role model! Parents please note.

NO SMOKING

I cannot leave the subject of parents and preparation without raising one issue. If either of your parents smoke, I strongly recommend you negotiate an agreement with them not to smoke

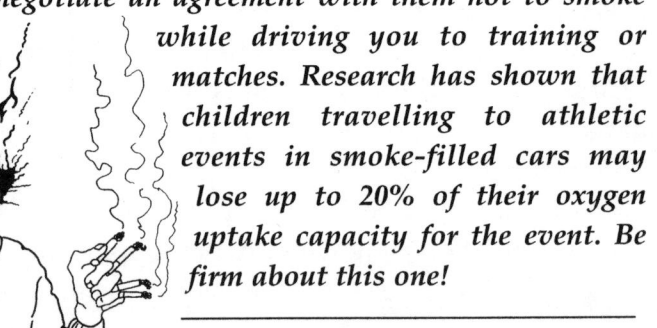

while driving you to training or matches. Research has shown that children travelling to athletic events in smoke-filled cars may lose up to 20% of their oxygen uptake capacity for the event. Be firm about this one!

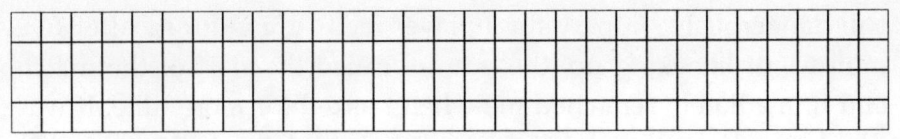

8 Managing Adults

Whose tennis is it anyway?
A parent or a coach must be experienced
as a support, not a threat.

Tough Choices

On one occasion I had reached the final in a
tournament that had been beset with bad
weather. It poured with rain just as my
match was due to start. The wait was
bad enough but then the
organisers wanted us to start
the final before the courts were
sufficiently dry. They were
notoriously slippery courts
when wet and other players had
already fallen or complained. There was
even a notice stating that the courts were
slippery when wet and that players play
at their own risk.

  We asked the organisers for a 15-minute
delay but they refused. They told me to try
the court in a knock-up. I did, and it was

still dangerously slippery for a player really going for it. After five minutes of knocking up, the umpire called the start of the match and immediately scratched me when I asked for more time. It was a bad mistake on the part of the organisers and it was disappointing for me, but is only one example of the sort of thing that may happen. An explanation for this incident follows, but let us first note that *adults can and do make mistakes. They also find it very difficult to admit their mistakes, especially to children.*

Don't Court Injuries

English weather is such that we often have to train on slippery courts in winter, but then you can choose how hard to play. A serious match is an entirely different matter, especially in the summer when the weather may quickly improve. Furthermore, many adults play tennis in a more leisurely way than we do and have little feel for the twists and turns of the junior competitive game. These people sometimes hold positions of authority in tennis and it is hard for a child to challenge them. However, there are enough injuries in junior tennis without asking for more. *You must take responsibility for yourself, don't expect others to.*

From the incident just described, I learned not to automatically submit to adults' agendas, and not to be afraid to withdraw from a match on safety grounds. To do so may even teach the offending adult something. No one match, not even a final, is going to spoil a tennis career, but an avoidable injury might! Safety and integrity to one's own principles are more important.

Tennis is a marathon not a match.

The day we learn that adults are not always right is an important one. For most of us it comes long before we pick up our first tennis

racket. Yet the belief, or is it hope, persists that they always know best, and they keep telling us that they do. I certainly believed for a long time that my first coach was right about tennis. Then another coach who I respected told me something technical that directly contradicted what I had been told before. I felt not only confused but let down. Then it dawned on me that there was an important lesson in this.

Coaches

Coaches are not always right. In fact, there is no absolute right in tennis technique nor, perhaps, in anything else, only a large number of often differing opinions. I began to realise that my opinion was valid too. Their opinion is based on their own knowledge and experience, but if knowledge differs then so can experience.

Your opinion will be based less on knowledge and past experience but more on present experience or what feels right for you and your body. Our senses served us well when we learned to walk, run and throw a ball or a Frisbee. Why should they not work for hitting a tennis ball? Listen to what coaches have to say, take it into account, and try it out; but your final judgement must be based on whether it feels right and whether it works for you. That is, after all, what Bjorn Borg did when he popularised the double-handed backhand and the high top spin baseline shot, and what Berasategui does when he hits his forehand and his backhand on the same side of his racket. They did all right doing it their own way.

Pay attention to your coaches' input but their way is not necessarily the only way. You must decide what is right for you.

Having said that, the quality of the coaches you have on your tennis journey, and in particular the quality of your relationship with them will determine both your technique and your enthusiasm for tennis. I say *coaches* because it is most unlikely for quite practical reasons such as location, availability and changing preferences, that you will remain with the same coach throughout your time in junior tennis.

Your coach needs to be your friend not an authority figure who reminds you of school. You need to be able to laugh and have fun with him or her. You need to respect each other enough for you to be willing to do some of the less exciting but necessary drills and exercises without whinging, and for the coach to listen to your opinions and understand when you are tired or having an off day.

I have been lucky enough to have had several coaches over the years who met these criteria but Heath Anthony and then John Shepherd have been outstanding. They always managed to make playing points against them a joy, a challenge and a learning experience all rolled into one. It is with John's guidance that I have made much progress recently and I am deeply grateful for his patience and his understanding of me and my game. I am not easy!

Your coach should, of course, be technically less competent and capable of hitting to a standard well above your own. This is not likely to be an issue until you are playing well in your mid-teens. Probably most important of all is that your coach has a genuine personal interest in your tennis development and success. This does not mean that he or she cannot also have the same concern for others, even those you compete against, but it does mean that they care to the extent that at times they show willing to help beyond what they charge you for.

For example, your coach may occasionally come and watch you play a match in order to give you some match-play feedback and guidance. This feels very supportive and may be very helpful. Encourage your coach to do it as much as they are able, and be grateful when they do. You can't expect them to do it too often if it is unpaid, and they will probably also have several other competition players to keep an eye on. However, for advanced players, match observation by the coach whenever possible should be a part of the established coach/player relationship.

Good coaches will encourage you to review a match with them even if they did not see it. And it is especially useful to video some of your matches for review later. Videoing a match may make another player nervous, so be sure to ask your opponent if he or she has any objection to someone videoing the match. Useful feedback also comes from another source.

Parental Feedback

Your parents will probably see you play more matches than anyone else will and can therefore give you good feedback, and they can do the videoing. Even if they do not know much about tennis, they will easily recognise your mental state and probably how it effected your physical performance. They may not always be absolutely right, but that is no reason to dismiss what they have to say. It will usually contain something you can learn from.

Parents will bring their own biases and blindness into their feedback. Mothers who think that everything their little darling does is perfect are unhelpful; so are fathers who see their child as a budding Pete Sampras or Martina Hingis from the age of four with their first swing of a plastic bat. Then there are those fathers who get angry every time you play because you are not perfect, could have done better, run faster, tried harder or at least won the last point. They will undermine your confidence and the accuracy of their criticisms is very suspect.

Fortunately, most parents, including yours I hope, fall between these two extremes.

However, there is always likely to be two problems. First, they will probably give their feedback in

a critical, mainly negative way and use phrases like: *you never* and *you always*; or in a prescriptive way: *you should have, you must*, etc. Secondly, even if they are not critical, you will probably think they are and become defensive about what they say anyway. What you need is objective feedback, match analysis and non-judgmental but empirical observations.

It took my dad and I some years before he could give me feedback in a way that I was willing to accept with an open mind. I never wanted advice before a match either and used to quickly say, 'I know, I know!' or 'I will, I will!' and then not do it anyway, which drove my dad crazy. I lost a lot of good learning opportunities through resisting my dad's input. Don't make the same mistake.

The timing of parental feedback should be agreed between you. Immediately after a match, win or lose, I did not want to talk about it, but it was fine some time later when the emotion associated with the match had subsided. If this is true for you, and it is for most young players, I recommend that you make an agreement about the timing with your parents, and then *be willing to listen, consider, and speak openly.*

How to Give and Get Feedback

The best method for a parent to provide feedback and advice is for them to use the coaching principles elaborated in chapters 9 and 10. In summary, they should hold back their own opinions at least at the beginning and ask the young player questions to elicit his or her experiences, views and concerns. The questions are to cause the player to review the match in their own mind in order to understand for themselves and to become accustomed to reviewing their play objectively, honestly and independently. Some examples of useful questions after a match are:

- *What did you do well during the match?*
- *How intense were you in the first few games?*
- *Where was your opponent gaining points against you?*
- *What area did you have least confidence in?*
- *What percentage of your first serves were in?*
- *If you had to play that opponent again, what would you do differently?*

This brings us to the questions to ask instead of giving advice. They will be questions which cause the player to visualise how they want to play:

- *What do you want to focus on?*
- *What tactics are you going to use?*
- *What are you going to do if the opponent quickly goes four games up?*
- *What are you going to do to maintain your intensity if you gain an easy early lead?*

Answering these questions causes the player to think and to be fully engaged. Their value does not depend on the parent having a high degree of tennis knowledge. Their purpose is to raise the player's *awareness* about the match they have just played or are about to play and, importantly, to get the player to take full *responsibility* for what happened or make their own choices about what will happen.

Parents Please Note

By all means give detailed descriptive, as opposed to judgmental, additional feedback from your observations, or advice from your knowledge or experience after the young player has had the opportunity to think about their play and talk it through for themselves. Any feedback or advice given prior to this reduces their potential for awareness and reduces the player's responsibility, and should therefore be avoided.

Finally, if no coach or parent is present there is absolutely no reason why the player cannot ask themselves the questions and attempt to answer them internally, fully and honestly. With a little practice, self-coaching is not difficult and can be used before, during, or after a match. It should not be confused with self-instruction or self-criticism which almost invariably lead to tension, frustration and, ultimately, failure.

Other Competitors' Parents

In the main they are very nice and friendly, remember your name, treat you well and are often helpful. Some *appear* nice, but they may try to undermine your confidence with the odd comment before your match against their beloved. A few will watch the match noisily querying your line calls and even actively endorsing your opponent's calls, fair or foul. These parents are thankfully rare but they will have trained their children to cheat by their example, if not deliberately. If your dad is bigger than your opponent's dad, he may add weight to your side of the argument! On second thoughts, it is better to hold your ground calmly and firmly and *call for an umpire if you need to*. A word of caution – amateur umpires may have defective eyesight and cause more trouble than they save!

Tennis Club Members

I have commented on officials, coaches and parents but there is another group of tennis adults who must be mentioned – the playing club members. Some of these people are understanding parents of young tennis players, others are very supportive of children's tennis, some just treat children like anyone else, others ignore children altogether, but a few are monsters. They are arrogant, snobbish and, what's more, mostly useless at tennis. They puff, pant and prance around playing pat-ball tennis. Their technique is atrocious and they look ridiculous, especially their serve which often consists of a wind up like Becker or McEnroe followed by a pause and a feeble tap high over the net!

What makes them so obnoxious? Is it the noise we make (they cannot stand our laughter or our grunting), our colourful tennis clothes, our occupation of *their* courts, or the fact that our technique is an ever-present reminder of their lack of it? They rarely complain directly to children on court, but make loud, snorting, caustic comments to one another about our very existence. The only way to deal with them is to carry on as usual, not get fazed by the comments and return their stray balls promptly and politely. It is a good exercise in mental control!

Friends of the Family

Here is another kind of adult irritation. Having listened to your parents enthusing about your tennis, their friends will often try to make relevant conversation with you by asking questions like, *'When are we going to see you at Wimbledon?'* I suppose it is well-meant, but it can be very tedious. *If I have heard it once, I have heard it a zillion times!*

Not only are such comments boring, but they can feel like a put-down. They suggest that getting to the top of tennis is easy and that any keen player can do it. Most adults outside tennis have no understanding of how demanding and tough getting to the top of junior tennis is – never mind Wimbledon! Yes, it is great fun, a privilege even, but it is no easy ride. I have not played tennis to the exclusion of all else and I have been fortunate to have had a lot of tennis at my present school, but I have not had time to do many of the fun things that less committed kids can choose to do. It is sometimes hard to remember that their silly question was well intentioned!

For reasons of their own, adults will also have opinions about our equipment and clothing.

Tennis Rackets

When you start playing tennis you are likely to want the latest Day-Glo green racket just like your best friend's. Someone probably told

you it is the best and you liked it when you borrowed it. Your parents will insist on giving you the orange one and will tell you it is even better. The truth is that it is probably cheaper. Disappointed as you may be, it really won't make any difference to your tennis in its early stages.

I know you will want to look good and have the best equipment, but you will soon discover that getting on in tennis depends more on playing better than on having a particular racket (T-shirt, cap, tennis shoes, etc.), although advertising and fashion freaks will try to convince you otherwise. The local sports shop will have an adequate selection of tennis gear for your first year or two. Later, the right racket for you with the right string and tension will be important, as will your choice of tennis shoes. Listen to all the advice you can get, then make your own choice by feel not by fashion.

Tennis Clothing

For some weird adult reason many tournaments, except Wimbledon, Roland Garros and the like, demand that we wear 'predominantly' white 'proper' tennis clothes – not T-shirts. The trouble is that every official interprets 'predominantly' and 'proper' differently. Recently, a friend of mine turned up at a tournament wearing the same type of shoe that Gustavo Kuerten wore to win the 1997 French Open. He was told that they were not tennis shoes and that they would damage the court! My genuinely proper tennis clothes have not always been acceptable either, so I take some all whites to change into if necessary, for there is little point in getting into a hassle about it. To do so is likely to take your focus off the match or get you unnecessarily emotionally charged.

A Brief Summary of Adult Behaviour

Adult tennis officials, organisers and umpires mean well but they can and do at times make mistakes. Junior tennis has changed much since they played, but they probably haven't. However, they do hold the power and are unlikely to back down. Don't let your frustration with their occasional unfairness spoil your play or your day.

Coaches may differ over technique. There is no one way to hit a tennis ball and your opinion and 'what feels right for you' needs to be respected. Your coach is your greatest resource, your friend and your support.

Parents may be critical but they can also be very helpful if you are willing to listen to them. An outside view is useful and they see more of your tennis than anyone else does. Encourage them to use a questioning technique with you. Tell them what your needs are. Avoid their smoke.

Other tennis parents are usually friendly but just occasionally your opponent's parents may not be quite as nice as they seem.

Tennis club members are generally harmless, even pleasant, but watch out for the exceptions! Don't trash them.

As a postscript to this chapter and to my section of this book and because every story should have a happy ending, I include the following. I was able to return to the Bollettieri Tennis Academy for two glorious weeks in October 1997 during the writing of this book. Coach De Palmer is Nick Bollettieri's right-hand man and one of the wise old men of tennis. All four of his children played high level tennis. In fact, his son Mike was Boris Becker's coach. My dad asked Mike, as both a top coach and a parent, what message he most wants to convey to aspiring young tennis stars. Without hesitation he took out a piece of paper and wrote this note.

My son, Mike De Palmer, Jr., after winning the Under 18 National Doubles Championships at Kalamazoo, Michigan, and I were attending the trophy awards ceremony and, as was the custom, I was asked to say a few words on behalf of all the tennis coaches/fathers in attendance. I recall saying, "The championship was indeed an honour, but tomorrow, he still had to cut the grass at home."

Mike De Palmer, Sr.

NICK BOLLETTIERI TENNIS ACADEMY

EXECUTIVE OFFICES

5500 34th STREET WEST
BRADENTON, FLORIDA 34210
PHONE (813) 755-1000
FAX (813) 758-0196

My son, Mike DePalmer, Jr., after winning the under 18 national Doubles Championships at Kalamazoo, Michigan, and I were attending the trophy awards ceremony, and as was the custom, I was asked to say a few words on behalf of all the tennis coaches/fathers in attendance. I recall saying, "The championship was indeed an honor, but tomorrow, he still had to cut the grass at home."

Mike DePalmer, Sr.

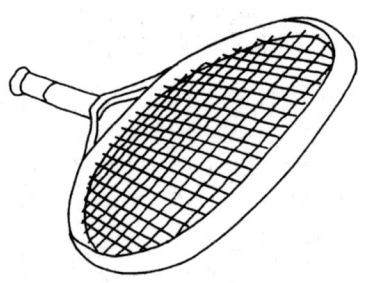

PART II

FOR ADVANCED JUNIOR TENNIS PLAYERS, THEIR PARENTS AND COACHES

JOHN WHITMORE

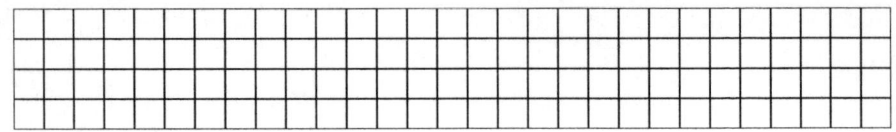

Introduction

The mind is key, but
who holds the key to your mind?

The *inner game* is a set of principles devolved into a method of coaching that is equally applicable to sport, business or life itself. It supersedes or, if that is too presumptive, complements traditional sports coaching and instruction. The history, principles and application of the inner game are described in detail in the next two chapters, but why have we included them in this book?

Two important distinguishing features of the inner game are particularly relevant to our subject. One is that inner game coaching works simultaneously on both the mental and the physical skills of tennis, and this will be useful for open-minded coaches trying to manage the volatile emotions of young competitors both on and off court. The second is that tennis expertise is not a prerequisite of successful inner game tennis coaching. This means that courageous parents can use it to support their children off court and even on it, and that dedicated juniors can self-coach when they are just hitting with a friend or when things turn sour in a match and help from coaches or parents is disallowed. The inner game provides coaches, parents and young players with a method of continuously attending to the mental side of the game without having to resort to a shrink.

In spite of its tennis origins, the inner game is used rarely in tennis but widely in business. Coaching in business is the inner game. In the past five years, coaching has become a buzz word in business parlance and a key skill for staff development. However, leading businesses have already moved one step further. Coaching, or the principles on which it is based, is seen to represent the management style of the emerging new business culture, or the future norm of people and performance management.

Business skill-development methods of the past or the old management styles, which have many similarities to conventional tennis teaching, are now seen as prescriptive, instructional, dictatorial, authoritarian or command and control – and as outmoded. Has business got it wrong, or been conned, or has sport, in this case tennis, some catching up to do? Let us examine how the inner game works and you can decide for yourself.

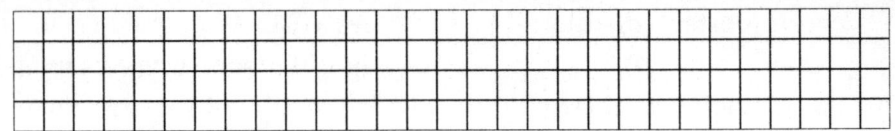

9 The Inner Game

Building Awareness and Responsibility is the essence of good coaching.

Traditionally, the teaching of all sports has consisted of an expert imparting his superior knowledge to his student through instruction and demonstration. Since the process seems logical and it works, few have thought to question it. However, one who did was Californian, Tim Gallwey. He was ranked among the top ten US national juniors in 1953 and went on to become captain of the Harvard Tennis team. In 1974 he wrote a book entitled *The Inner Game of Tennis* which challenged both the logic and the effectiveness of orthodox tennis teaching, and it became a huge bestseller.

His starting point was that the mind plays a far greater part in the game than had previously been acknowledged. The struggle that all players experience with trying too hard, with self-criticism and condemnation, with lapses in concentration and with muscular tension caused by the foregoing, is what he called the inner game. He pointed out something that few of us can deny, 'that the opponent within our own head is more formidable than the one on the other side of the net.'

Gallwey further suggested that if we learn to master the inner game, the outer game of hitting furry balls over the net into the court and winning the last point of the match, develops naturally and easily.

Gallwey grew up in California in the 1960s, in the place and at the time when old behaviourist psychology, on which traditional teaching was based, was first being superseded by humanistic and transpersonal psychological thinking. *The Inner Game of Tennis* pioneered the application of new thought to an old game, but it will still take a generation or two for long- established methods based on old and flawed psychology to finally pass away.

Although, today the majority of coaches and good players are quick to acknowledge that winning at tennis or any other sport is *all in the mind*, mental training for juniors remains minimal and rudimentary. They may receive a lecture or two from a sports psychologist but not all coaches are equipped to address the vital mental and emotional aspects of the game with any sophistication. Unfortunately, *show and tell* continues to be the predominant method of tennis teaching even though it often runs counter to recent understanding about the inseparability of mental and physical skill development. Ideally, every time a coach goes on court he or she should fulfil the roles of both traditional tennis teacher and sports psychologist. This is what the inner game coach does and is what I believe true coaching really involves.

The public devoured *The Inner Game of Tennis* in unprecedented numbers because Gallwey was the first to put his finger on the mental struggles we have, both on and off court. However, it is one thing to recognise a problem in ourselves but quite another to be able to help others to deal with it in themselves. In his book, Gallwey did not attempt to tell coaches how to address the mental obstacles of their charges. And because he was so concerned with quality control he was even reluctant to train other coaches to do what he did so well. He knew it would take time, dedication and the abandonment of some traditional tennis thinking on the part of the trainee coach, and that many would never make the transition. It came easier to me as I was not a tennis coach, or even a player, so I had less to give up. Tim trained me in 1979, and I founded the Inner Game organisation in England.

While Tim's policy worked in one way, it led to another problem. There is a common human tendency to take a cursory glance at new ideas, assume we understand them, compare how they fit with our present thinking, and dismiss them if they seem too challenging. From a superficial reading of *The Inner Game of Tennis*, or a single experience of it in action in the early days, many people in the tennis establishment made some false assumptions. This lead to wrongly executed attempts to apply the principles and often ended in failure. They usually blamed *The Inner Game* instead of themselves and never gave it a second look. Gallwey was ahead of the times, but now change is in the air. Despite having been dismissive of inner game principles in the past, some of the best coaches from other sports are beginning to employ similar methods.

For the sake of clarity the inner game approach can be broken down into three realms. Gallwey did not make such divisions, and in practice all three are addressed simultaneously. They are as follows:

1. The most visible realm of the inner game is what much of this book has been about, *how to deal with the upsets, the lapses in concentration, the over-caution and other mental interferences* that juniors frequently experience on court. It includes how to think differently about winning and losing, how to remain in the here-and-now and how to deal with pressures and disappointments on and off court.

2. The second realm of the inner game is this. Traditional coaching methods have always been based on the belief that higher standards of physical fitness and better technique lead to better performance. As far as technique is concerned, the *cure* is seen as further explanation, demonstration and practice of the correct technique. Indeed, frequent repetition may instil technique to some extent and under favourable conditions. However, the greater problem is the *inability to apply optimum technique, rather than a lack of knowledge of it*. The causes of this inability lie in the

mind of individual players and vary widely among them. The inner game seeks to address these.

3. The third realm of the inner game is less well understood and is perhaps more challenging to traditionalists, and yet it is one that has great potential for coaches and for performance improvement. The challenge lies in the answer to the question, *What are coaches trying to achieve – correct technique or optimum bio-mechanical efficiency?* Correct tennis technique is traditionally instilled from outside by an expert, but real *bio-mechanical efficiency depends on the quantity and quality of feedback from internal kinaesthesis (the sensation by which bodily position, weight, muscle tension and movement are perceived).* The inner game coach seeks to enhance a player's own kinaesthetic feedback to generate the optimum technique for each individual – from the inside out. Since no two bodies are identical, bio-mechanical efficiency is going to appear outwardly or technically different for each individual. *Technique imported from the outside in is never custom made, but that evoked from within, always is.* More about this realm later.

Realm number one has been extensively addressed throughout this book, so, let's consider number two by looking at a couple of examples to illustrate the point.

Inability to Apply Technique: Volley

Recently, I watched a 13-year-old girl playing a doubles match. She hit her cross court ground strokes aggressively and well but up at the net her tennis broke down. The normal prescription would have been more volley practice: 'keep your wrist firm... don't let the racket head drop... punch the volley... continue to move forward,' etc. I'll bet she had heard it all a hundred times and probably done it in practice, but she was unable to apply it during the match.

It was clear the problem was not one of technique, but in a match any potential volley represented a threat to her rather than an opportunity to win the point. She did not want her opponents to hit the ball within her reach and when they did, what did she do? She retreated, she even closed her eyes momentarily, her wrist went soft, her racket head dropped and she punched nothing. Her technique failed because of her fear. Further technical training will have a very limited effect until her fear is addressed.

An inner game coach would instantly recognise this and work on her fear by asking her questions to raise her self-awareness.

- *What is it exactly that you are afraid of?*
- *So it is failure or another mistake – how serious is that really?*
- *Even if your doubles partner gets upset with you – how serious is that?*
- *What body sensations do you experience when you are fearful?*
- *What are the effects of your fear on you and your game?*

And add a proactive question or two, such as:
- *What do you need to do to overcome this?*

Then, during a practice session further questions would be asked:
- *How close to your racket is the ball when you take your eyes off it as it comes towards you?*
- *What movements do you make the instant you see a volley coming?*

- *How firm is your wrist on a 1–10 scale just prior to contact, on contact, etc.?*

Once this player becomes aware of her emotions about volleying and her actual physical responses as they occur, both will begin to change for the better – she will self-correct. Later, she can learn to ask herself the questions, first in practice then in matches if necessary. Most importantly for her, she will discover how to learn and begin to experience self-mastery or self-responsibility, as well as how to volley with confidence.

Inability to Apply Technique: Second Serve

Let us take an example of a different stroke, the serve and in particular the double fault. Many young players rush their second serve. They have been told repeatedly not to but they still do, and telling them yet again is pointless. It is equally ineffective to give them yet more technical instructions on how to achieve a better serve, such as, 'Toss your ball higher on the second serve'. The ball toss is too low because they are rushing it, not because they don't know how high the ball toss should go. They are in too much of a hurry to notice how low it is. The thoughts and emotions that cause the rush, block their awareness. When these are resolved, their awareness returns and self-correction is automatic.

So, why do they rush the second serve? It is often because, unconsciously, they want to quickly cover up the fault of the first. This means they have not accepted and do not want to accept the mistake, so it stays with them and they are likely to repeat it. How many times have you seen a second serve follow exactly the same path into the net as the first? The player's mind retains the visual memory of the first serve failure and, not surprisingly, the second serve conforms to the same picture.

Sometimes, a server will overcompensate, overcorrect and hit the second serve long. This also occurs because they are mentally holding on to the first serve and trying to correct the result of that one rather than use the correct process for the next. Learning how to let go of the first serve is essential. Inner game coaching questions will take the player away from the *there and then* and back to the *here and now*. Then the service ritual can be created from the start and include a new visualisation of where the ball is to go.

Most conventional tennis coaches know that it works to slow down the time between serves and will try to get their pupils to do so. However, because they don't understand the root cause of the problem, they try to solve it by instructing for *behaviour* which is less effective and less permanent than coaching away the underlying *attitude* or *anxiety*.

What these two examples illustrate is that what appear to be technical errors actually often stem from the mental state of the player and therefore any permanent resolution of them must be made in the mind. Technical quick fixes will last till the end of the lesson, or the end of the month, perhaps, but that is not good enough. If you follow the logic of these examples, might it not be true that the majority of technical errors have their origins in the mind of the player and therefore that is where they must be addressed?

When we remove the mental obstacles, the technique and therefore the performance will optimise. This principle is closely related to that which governs the third part of the inner game. Take away the bio-mechanical inefficiencies, and the technique and performance will optimise.

Before we examine this one in more detail, it may help to restate and enlarge upon the core principles, assumptions and beliefs on which inner game coaching is based, and illustrate how we work with them.

Core Principles

Our performance is our potential diminished by our internal interferences. The inner game aims to eliminate or at least reduce these interferences. Winning the inner game, thereby optimising mental and physical skill development, requires the underlying belief by the coach and the player that we all have far greater potential to perform and to learn, both mentally and physically, than we commonly manifest. The way to access our latent potential is through high *Awareness* and *Responsibility*.

Awareness is defined as 'self-accessed, high quality, relevant input', which means that a player's awareness is gained through observation, tactile and kinaesthetic sensing, and mental and emotional self-monitoring.

Responsibility in players is their sense of total ownership of what happens to them and what they do. It is developed by being offered choice, a key to self-reliance, self-esteem and self-motivation and by being invited to respond to awareness-raising coaching questions.

How they work

If a player becomes aware of a weakness in their game, there is a natural tendency to correct it consciously, or for it to self-correct, unconsciously. Conversely, if a player remains unaware of a flaw, it is unlikely to change. Normal instruction is based on the principle that an expert says what is being done wrong and what should be done instead. The player is then expected to make a conscious correction. This works, but only to a degree because true awareness is not achieved by being told something. Information at the level of intellect alone does not equate with awareness. Awareness comes from the senses too.

- *Awareness is knowing what is going on.*
- *Self-awareness is knowing what you are experiencing.*
- *Awareness is knowing what you are doing.*
- *High levels of awareness have an almost magical quality – and effect.*
- *Awareness itself is curative.*

Awareness is what you recognise, discover, feel, and observe for yourself, as opposed to what you read or are told. In fact, being told something actually relieves a person of the need to pay sufficient attention to find out for themselves. Telling them takes that opportunity and responsibility away from them.

Some traditional teachers reject inner game principles because they fear the *apparent* loss of authority and control. They do not want to *give* responsibility to the learner. However, it is taking on this responsibility that brings to the young tennis player an accumulative building of self-awareness, self-reliance, self-management, self-esteem, self-confidence and self-motivation. All these mental skills are essential for any sports performer, and are the bedrock of mental and emotional stability in a tennis match.

Besides, the inner game makes no injunction *never* to tell. There are occasions when it is entirely appropriate to do so. For example, when asked to tell by a player, or when a player who is usually strong on self-responsibility occasionally just wants a quick answer. Endless questions will drive most young players crazy, anyway. But, we should always bear in mind that *telling* **reduces** *awareness and responsibility.*

Correct Technique or Optimum Bio-Mechanical Efficiency?

Here we address the third realm of the inner game.

An inner game coach does not immediately point out a player's flaws, but asks questions that cause them to pay particular attention to an area (usually one they have chosen themselves) of their game, stroke or body, and thereby to recognise any inefficiency occurring in those areas. Correction follows naturally and effortlessly. For example, a physical discomfort indicates a bio-mechanical inefficiency in the body or in a movement. In our normal daily lives when we feel or experience a discomfort, we automatically and often subconsciously make subtle changes to the movement to rid ourselves of the discomfort. We, in fact, restore or improve the bio-mechanical efficiency of the action.

This natural process of self-correction is evoked through heightened awareness during the physical actions of sport. An improvement in technique results because *technique is actually no more than using our body in its most efficient way to achieve a given objective.* Furthermore, since no two bodies are identical, the optimum technique will vary for each person and cannot be prescribed.

Your physique and your technique must be perfectly compatible if you are to perform at your full potential.

The outsider, the instructor, the expert, cannot see another person's level of discomfort or bio-mechanical inefficiency. They can only observe his or her technique and make general judgements about its efficiency from their knowledge and past experience. Even if the judgement or advice is good, imposing either of them reduces the responsibility of the player. It must be considered whether that is a worthwhile trade off, given the value of building and maintaining player responsibility. It *may* be, but we must also remember that any correction is an assumption and a generalisation and is likely to be inferior to the subtle subconscious self-correction that occurs naturally if the player applies sufficiently high awareness to the feel of the action. Conscious correction often overcompensates or throws other components of an action out of time or out of balance, whereas subconscious correction by sensory awareness integrates holistically.

Why then do we not do everything, including play tennis, quite naturally in the most efficient way? Surely we do not enjoy discomfort? Why do we need coaches at all?

Unfortunately, our normal level of awareness is relatively low; let us say only 25% of what is attainable with practice and focus. It is a good thing it is low; if it were higher we would probably become obsessed with the multitude and magnitude of our own sensations. Much of the time, bio-mechanical inefficiencies or discomfort exist but are below our normal awareness threshold. This is no disadvantage when we go about our day-to-day activities but it is when we want to produce higher levels of performance, as we do if we are serious about our sport.

To improve our bio-mechanical efficiency, we need to be far more aware than normal while training. With practice, our awareness or sensitivity level can rise considerably. Extreme awareness not only produces high efficiency, but also it may lead to an extraordinary state of relaxed concentration in which actions seem to take place in slow motion. Sports performers, occasionally, and people during an accident quite frequently experience this state. However, this is not a realistic goal of raising our awareness, but it does serve to illustrate the extremes of awareness that exist.

Coach or Expert?

It may have become apparent by now that while inner game coaches need to be highly skilled at questioning, they are not dependent on the skill, knowledge or experience of tennis. Rather than being teachers, they are in effect awareness raisers who cause players to pay more attention and become more aware as they themselves seek or sense answers. This different function opens the door for some parents to assist their children by coaching them, and for young players to self-coach. With a little practice, children can become quite skilled at asking themselves effective awareness-raising questions to improve their physical efficiency at tennis without the aid of a tennis expert or even an external coach.

This concept may be seen as a surprise, a heresy or even a threat by some *experts*. Most people who teach tennis will, of course, have tennis expertise, which eliminates that problem but raises another. For *tennis experts* to employ this coaching method rather than instruct, demands considerable self-discipline. It is hard to resist the temptation to tell, which is the easy option for those who think they know all the answers, but the benefits of holding back are great.

I have often been asked why, if I am such an advocate of inner game coaching, I am not Jason's coach. I have coached him on occasion, particularly on his serve, but I have never been and would never be his coach for many reasons. I do not play tennis and therefore am unable to hit balls with him. We would have to bring in a hitter. I cannot always be available at the times he wants coaching. He needs at least to be engaged with the established tennis system for practical reasons. However, and most importantly, I firmly believe that the role of a supportive parent and the role of principle tennis teacher should be separate. There are successful examples of these roles being combined but in my opinion it raises a number of conflict-of-interest issues that are better avoided.

The next chapter further illustrates how to apply inner game principles and how to formulate effective coaching questions, using the particular but crucially important area of *keeping your eye on the ball* as but one other example of their many possible applications.

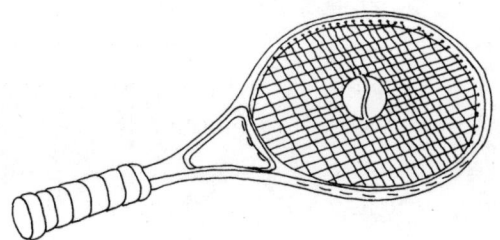

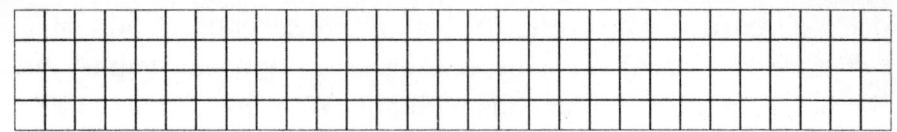

10 Keep Your Eye on the Ball

*I am able to control only what
I am aware of.*

'Keep your eye on the ball,' is probably the most used and least useful instruction ever given in tennis. Many commands of a similar kind are equally common and equally unproductive. To suggest that the everyday fare of ball sports is fundamentally flawed may seem arrogant and presumptive, but before you leap to such a conclusion, I invite you to follow the argument, try out the suggestions that follow, and judge for yourself.

Make no mistake, keeping your eye on the ball is probably the single most important thing you can do. Far from challenging that, I will be emphasising its value. However, what I assert is that the command, 'Keep your eye on the ball,' will not cause you to do so, and that there is a more effective method of achieving it.

- *If you are asked to say which way the ball is spinning each time it comes towards you, you will not be able to answer unless you focus on the ball.*
- *If you are asked where the name of the ball manufacturer is each time your racket makes contact with it, you will be obliged to watch the ball right on to the racket.*
- *If you are asked which way or how fast the ball spins after it bounces, this will also ensure your focus follows the ball.*
- *If you are asked how high over the net the ball passes after it leaves your racket you will get accurate feedback of the results of your action.*
- *If you are asked how close the ball is to your opponent's racket when you first recognise the direction of spin (from the ball, not the stroke), you will see the ball just as it leaves your opponent, and therefore receive earlier directional input.*
- *If you are asked where the approaching ball is in relation to the net at the moment you make your decision about where on the court you are going to hit it, you will learn something about your tactics, as well as keeping your eye on the ball. In fact, by merely noticing this you may find your decision making will be delayed, making it harder for your opponent to read your intentions.*

You cannot avoid watching the ball if you are to respond out loud to any of these questions. In other words, they compel you to watch the ball in a way that saying, 'Keep your eye on the ball,' does not. But these questions do far more than that. They cause you to focus to a higher degree than normal in order to acquire the additional detail the coach is calling for. This in turn provides you with higher than normal quality and quantity of information about the precise direction, speed and trajectory of the ball. Your mind/body system will automatically process this and thereby respond better. The questions keep the responsibility for the answers where it needs to be – with the player. And the answers provide coaches with feedback that they can compare with their own observations to determine the quality of the player's attention, and therefore what the next question should be.

Multiple Effects

The performance improvement produced by keeping your eye so sharply on the ball in tennis, or any other ball game, is outstanding. Timing improves, hits are better centred, footwork and positioning are improved due to earlier response, the head remains down during the shot due to the intense focus on the ball, the body is more fluid due to the relaxed concentration evoked. Several technical and tactical improvements come about simply through watching the ball better. And if the coach asks the questions often enough in practice, watching the ball so intently becomes a habit in practice and matches. All these effects result from the use of effective ball awareness-raising questions in place of the usual instructor's favourite command, 'Watch the ball!'.

And Applications

Of course, as suggested in the previous chapter, the same type of awareness-raising questions can equally be addressed to all other aspects of tennis, not just ball watching. There is racket awareness, opponent awareness, court awareness, tactical awareness, emotional awareness and perhaps the most important of all for power and efficient stroke production, kinaesthetic body awareness (see page 102).

For Coaches

The benefits of high awareness are not confined to beginner or intermediate players. I have seen seasoned professionals get high on the unexpected results they have experienced with their own tennis. On one occasion, after I had used some ball-watching questions with a coach he began to hit the ball exceptionally well. He turned to me and said, 'I realise now that I have never really watched the ball before, although I have been telling others to do so for ten years.'

Why on earth then do tennis and other sports coaches and instructors all over the world continue to use commands such as, 'Watch the ball,' to such poor effect? The answer is they have never thought to question the way they were taught. It is quick and easy, it is what they want the player to do, and they probably think there is no other way. Sadly, the tennis establishment in Britain and in America suffers from being fairly closed to new ideas, and yet traditionalists are often surprised by how effective they are when they finally get around to trying them out. This is an invitation to coaches, parents and young players to experiment for yourselves with the drills, and with your own variations on the principles. Here are some guidelines.

Effective Questions

From the examples I have given so far, it can be seen that the coaching interventions were all questions. However, not all questions are effective. For example, 'Are you watching the ball?' or 'Why are you not watching the ball?' are ineffective. They do not meet the criteria for effective questions which are as follows:

- They must be *open questions*.
- They must *compel* the player to pay *attention*.
- They must demand a *higher* degree of focus, detail and *precision* than normal.
- They must provide a *feedback loop* to the coach.

It can be seen that all the tennis questions on pages 86 and 113 meet three or all of these criteria. They are open, they compel attention, they call for detail, and in most cases the coach can compare what he sees with what the player reports. It can also be seen that the instruction, 'Keep your eye on the ball', meets *none* of these criteria which is probably why it does *not* work!

Bounce-Hit

This ball-watching exercise was also created by Tim Gallwey. It does not involve a question – not all coaching interventions have to be questions – but it is based on the same criteria. The player is told to say *bounce* the instant the ball touches the court in front of them, and *hit* the instant it meets the racket. Doing so, of course, causes the player to watch the ball on its approach right onto the racket. The secret is to focus on saying it exactly on time, so the words coincide precisely with the events. The player and/or the coach needs to monitor the timing closely or it can degenerate into saying words by rote that bear no relationship to the events.

The coach may also ask the player to call out *bounce* and *hit* in time with his hitting partners actions on the other side of the net. That causes the player to watch the ball all the way to and from the opponent's racket. We often get footwork improvements with this drill, as well as with other effective questions specific to footwork. This version of *bounce-hit* is especially effective with little children and beginners. I have seen many a player go instantly from two-ball to twenty-ball rallies simply by both players calling *bounce* and *hit* continuously on either side of the net. This is very exciting and encouraging for child beginners to whom early success is so important if they are to stay in the game.

The same principle can be applied to watching the ball on the serve, smash or volley by having the player say *now* the instant the ball touches the racket. In serving, asking how many centimetres (or inches) the ball drops before contact, causes the server to watch the ball right onto the racket and works wonders for the ball toss.

Hit-bounce can be used for serving practice to get the player to see the ball on contact *(hit)*. By asking them to say *bounce* the instant the ball touches the court or the net, the player receives accurate feedback about where the ball goes. It also prevents servers looking away and not accepting feedback from a ball they know is not going where they wanted it to. That feedback, if made non-judgmentally and it will be if it is obtained in this way, is just as useful as feedback from the successful shots.

Summary

Telling yourself or others to 'Keep your eye on the ball', does not work. *Bounce-hit* or asking the right questions, does. Learn to ask yourself or others effective questions that result in watching the ball throughout its flight or some particular aspect of it, depending on the results sought. Keeping your eye on the ball, really watching it with precision and detail, can work wonders for your tennis. The high quality focus generated in this way induces a state of relaxed concentration that eliminates other distractions and loosens the body to perform at its very best, as well as an intensity that will optimise court speed and racket timing. It is so simple and effective. Do work with it.

For those who wish to learn more about coaching in sport, and in business, I suggest you read my book *Coaching for Performance* (Nicholas Brealey Publishing); and I highly recommend that all tennis children, parents and coaches read *The Inner Game of Tennis* by Tim Gallwey (Pan Books).

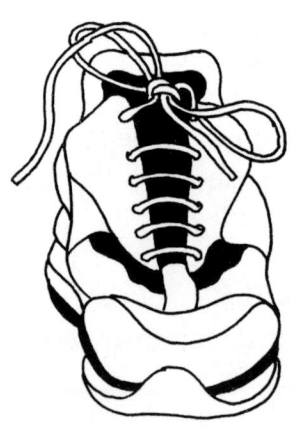

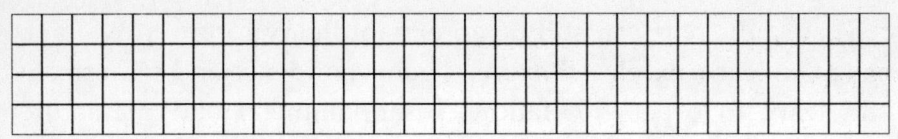

Conclusion

Tennis is a game, and games are for fun.

A Parental Perspective

More and more children are getting the opportunity and being encouraged to take up a sport seriously at ever younger ages. For some, this may turn out to be an important contribution towards eventual success in their chosen sport. However, it may place upon others demands and pressures that narrow their vision, limit their other experiences and opportunities and prevent them from having a natural and carefree childhood with all the benefits of being just a regular kid.

The driving forces are a conspiracy for success between the governing body of the particular sport, commercial interests, and the projected desires of parents. These factors often override or shape the wishes of the child to the extent that the child may not know or dare say what he or she really wants. They can be swept along by events and further pushed by peer group pressure and their own natural or adopted competitiveness. They enter a tournament because they did the last one and are expected to do the next. At times the sporting child's life style seems to be little more than an unhealthy reflection of the rat race in which some parents also engage, either willingly or unwillingly.

That said, sport can still be an extraordinary forum in which a child can learn, excel, self-express, gain confidence and self-esteem and learn to cope with failure, disappointment and premature success. It may take an adult decades to learn about life the things a child in sport can learn in a year. It will not be without casualties of a short term physical or even temporary psychological nature. On balance, I suspect that the majority of talented kids benefit greatly from their sporting experiences in early life and will look back upon even the toughest moments with pride and nostalgia. Only a tiny minority of the most dedicated ever find their way into professional sport after their teen years. In fact, even national champions at fourteen more often than not are forgotten by the time they are eighteen.

At a tennis tournament in which our sons were competing, ex British Davis Cup captain Paul Hutchens and I were musing about the future. I commented that nationally there were probably some two hundred children in their age group who had the raw capability of getting to the very top in tennis. I wondered how many of them would even get onto the Association of Tennis Professionals (ATP) tour circuit. My guess was two. Paul thought for a while and then said in a quiet and resigned voice, 'Probably none.'

I write this here not to discourage but because I feel that neither parents nor children should be under any illusion about what they are getting into. Many convince themselves that they are different, that they are the exception for this or that reason. It keeps parents trekking their kids all over the country to competitions and spending ludicrous amounts of money on the very best equipment when the second best would have been more than adequate.

It is easy to become cynical about the distortions of children's sporting mini-stardom, but Jason and I are deeply grateful for having had the opportunity to participate (something denied to many) and for the multiple benefits that accrue and accumulate from high level competitive experience. Sport is the luxury school of hard knocks for the privileged and the unreasonably dedicated. Making it to the very top is a huge bonus for the one who does, but the many less publicised victories of the others are often triumphs on the path of life when measured by personal, individual or spiritual criteria.

Tennis is only a game, but a great one to learn – and a great one to learn from.

ACKNOWLEDGEMENTS

It is easy for a young person who is enjoying a good life to take a lot for granted, but I have much to be grateful for and many people to thank very sincerely.

Caroline Harris gave me my first few tennis lessons; Clint Harris, my first coach, instilled in me some technique and tactics; the Kent County Squads helped to keep me on my toes; Heath Anthony made tennis fun and made me go for it; Andy Burgoyne taught me to serve, and John Shepherd my current coach combines fun, serious tennis and real support in an ideal way for me.

In America, Caesar and Alan Alvistur, Tim Gallwey, Chris Garner, Dave Herman and Jack Groppel all contributed to my tennis. Too many people to name at Nick Bollettieri's in Florida restored my enthusiasm for tennis after a low period, taught me what fun it was to work hard, and were exceptionally generous and supportive when an injury sadly cut short my stay. I thank Percy Melzi, especially for his kindness, care and attention to detail when coaching me.

Sevenoaks School, Charles Bailey and James Andell, and my doubles partner Will Shaw give me court, hitting, squad and match time. In helping my friend Barnaby Lucas with his tennis, I learned a lot about my own. Both my parents have unconditionally and unfailingly supported me through the good and the bad times in tennis and life.

For this book my dad worked hard to make sense and order of my experiences, writing, rewriting and editing them, and adding his own. The May, Evans and Alexander tennis families read a draft and gave us helpful advice, as did Jacob Rasmussen and sports psychologist Chris Harwood. Barry Cunningham of Element Children's Books courageously initiated the project and Helen Wire meticulously edited it. Dave Pitchford is not just a cartoonist, an artist and an entertainer, but is also the ultimate odd job man. He even put a spade through the main electricity cable to our house, but we managed to reconnect the computer and this book is the result.

Jason Whitmore

USEFUL ADDRESSES

The Lawn Tennis Association
The Queen's Club, West Kensington
London W14 9EG UK

National Training Centre
& Rover/LTA School
Bisham Abbey, Marlow
Buckinghamshire UK

The All England Lawn Tennis Club
Church Road, Wimbledon
London SW19 5AE UK

International Tennis Federation
Palliser Road, Barons Court
London W14 9EN UK

The United States Tennis Association
70 West Red Oak Lane
White Plains
New York
NY 10604

LGE Sports Science, Inc
9757 Lake Nona Road
Orlando, Florida 32827

Bollettieri Sports Acadamy
5500 34th Street West
Bradenton, Florida 34210

The Inner Game of Tennis
Sean Brawley, Director of Tennis
Spanish Hills Golf & Country Club
99 Crestview Avenue
Camarillo, California 93010